IMAGES OF ENGLAND

THE DINGS
AND ST PHILIPS

IMAGES OF ENGLAND

THE DINGS
AND ST PHILIPS

DAVE STEPHENSON AND JILL WILLMOTT

TEMPUS

Frontispiece: The Shaftesbury Crusade, Kingsland Road, 1970s.

First published 2005

Tempus Publishing Limited
The Mill, Brimscombe Port,
Stroud, Gloucestershire, GL5 2QG
www.tempus-publishing.com

British Library Cataloguing in Publication Data.
A catalogue record for this book is available from the British Library.

ISBN 0 7524 3556 6

Typesetting and origination by Tempus Publishing Limited.
Printed in Great Britain.

Contents

Acknowledgements

We gratefully acknowledge the help from the following in preparing this book: Shirley Norman, Simon Munden, Tony Stallard, Alan Kingdom, Delphine Higgs, Beth Trimmer, David M. Woods, George and Doreen Toop, David Toop, Tony Brake, Valerie Britton, Dot Tranter, Mary and Keith Wilson, John Merrett, W.H. Lucas, Len Chirton, Pete Moreman, Dennis Stinchcombe, John Penny, Jean Brake, Janet and Derek Fisher, Johnny Ratcliffe, Beryl Butler, J.M. Carter, Gary Knight, George Stone, Tony Filer, Dolores Powell, R.B. Leonard, David Cheesley, Garry Atterton, Lisa Vaughan, Marilyn Silverthorne, Pauline Luscombe, Jack Phelps, David Foot, Maurice Bye, the Smart Family, Barton Hill History Group, William Gregor, *Bristol Evening Post*, Bristol Record Office, Audrey McGrath, Robin Williams.

Special thanks to Dennis Stephenson (drawings), Brian Davies (St Philips Marsh historian), the late David Harrison (Editor, *Evening Post*), Andy Jones (local historian), S. Luxton, Mike Tozer, Marjorie Sheppard (*née* Hancock), Benjamin Price and George Toop who both helped to preserve the memory of The Dings, and Gerry Brooke, Editor of *The Bristol Times*, for his help and assistance.

Bibliography

Bridgeman, Geoff; *The story of the Jacob Street Brewery;* Journal of the Brewery History Society, 1995
Gregor, William; *Dings in the 1920s;* 1996
Kelly's Directory, 1994
Linton, Keith and Alan; *I will build my church*
Nabb, Harold; *The British Gas Industry;* Alan Sutton Publishing Ltd, 1987
Price, Benjamin; *A Tipplers Tale*; Sidney Alley Press, 1994
Somerville, John; *Soapmakers of Bristol*; White Tree Books, 1991

Introduction

The words of Benjamin Price, The Dings historian:

> In that time they created their own world, language, customs and way of life,
> I shall be, till the end of my days, eternally grateful to the fate which decided
> I should be born into The Dings, and its people. Life was not easy. Poverty,
> gut grinding poverty, was endemic; the illnesses and affliction of that poverty
> served with perversity to create a community in which tolerance, good nature
> and a will to survive and help others to survive, became a way of life.

The name 'Dings' is probably an old Anglo-Saxon word meaning 'the meadow
where withies grow'. Withies were used for making baskets. On old maps of
the area it is recorded as 'Dengs' or 'Dings'. When John Wesley, the founder of
Methodism, came to Bristol in 1739 to preach, one of the first places he visited
was St Philips. Wesley preached in the open air near the local brickyards as there
were no buildings large enough to hold a congregation in the area. He was to do
this throughout Bristol and Kingswood in order to reach the people who needed
him most

The area, at that time, consisted of barley fields, orchards and pastureland. Later
these fields were to be turned into market gardens. Around these smallholdings
were glass and pottery cones which would have been seen in Avon Street. There
were also soap boilers and hoopers. Later would come the iron works, lead and
paint works and in 1819, the gas works.

One of the oldest roads in the district is Barton Road. In 1739 this was a farm
track known as Cookes Lane.

The Feeder Canal was cut between 1804 and 1809, dividing the area in two
and separating it from the marsh, but giving the river a permanent high tide. Later
the Great Western Railway was to cut through many of the dwellings in the area.

The Phoenix glassworks, founded by Benjamin Lund, was taken over by Messrs
Wadham, Ricketts & Co. in 1789. It later became Powell, Ricketts & Co. and was
converted into a glass bottle manufactory, including the glass marbles used to seal
lemonade bottles. Children would collect these to play marbles in the street. This
factory closed in July 1923.

In 1835 the railway, horse drawn at first, came to St Philips. It ran from the district to the Coalpit Heath coalmines. It was later amalgamated into the Midland line. Stothert's were in the district making locomotives. They later became known as the Avonside Works and moved to fishponds in 1905. There was also Lysaght's steelworks and Butler's ironworks in Silverthorne Lane. Butler's also had works at Crews Hole. Gardiner, still very much in evidence today, started in Nelson Street but by 1897 they had opened the Midland Road ironworks. In 1953 they took over the old soap factory premises to expand the business. In 1865, Derham's built a large seven-storey factory to make boots and shoes in Barton Street. It was destroyed by fire in 1905. The business was bought by the Steadman family, who had a long connection with the Shaftesbury Crusade, and finally by the firm of Spear Bros & Clark Ltd, who had a sausage and pie factory in Broad Plain.

What must be asked is, would all of these firms have set up business in St Philips if, as someone once wrote, 'evil of every description stalked the streets and alleyways unashamed'? Despite the police station in Trinity Road, fairly close to the old prison, a pub on almost every corner meant fights and trouble of all sorts and the police only walked the streets in pairs.

It was religion that was to change the face of The Dings. Within a few years there were churches, chapels and mission halls of every denomination, The Salvation Army made valiant efforts to tempt the drunken from the pubs by preaching outside. They later had premises in Unity Street, and were allowed to use the upstairs of Cooksley ironmongers as a meeting place, which held 1,200 people. They also built places to worship in Lawrence Hill and Easton. In the end there was almost a chapel or a church in every street, co-existing with the local pubs. The Shaftesbury Crusade opened its doors and became the true heart of the community. Broad Plain Boys' Club also provided very good sporting facilities for the youth of the area.

After half a century of neglect, The Dings area is being restored to a useful life again.

Dave Stephenson and Jill Willmott
March 2005

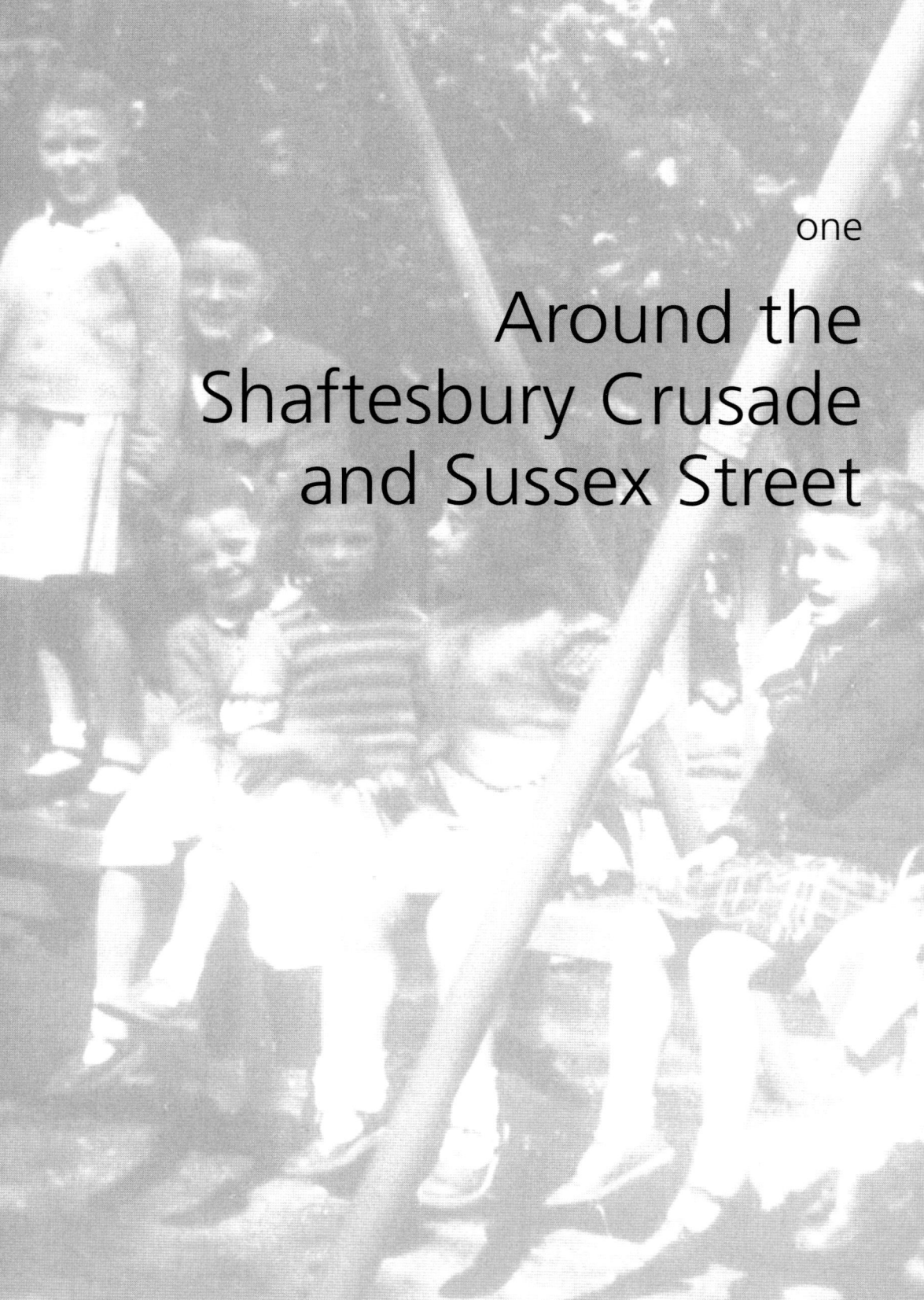

one

Around the Shaftesbury Crusade and Sussex Street

The Shaftesbury Crusade started life as a Christian and social mission in the appalling slums of St Philips and The Dings. In 1852 it was reported that 'a dense and almost impenetrable brown mist masks the grimy, filthy and hovel-crowded district of The Dings, where labour and squalor have shaken hands and made contact together to withstand the opposing forces of civilisation and comfort.'

The Shaftesbury was founded by Dr Bell who had also founded the nearby Cumberland Street Mission. Other leaders came mainly from Redland Park church, namely Mr Wilberforce Tribe, Mr E. Robinson, Mr J.H. Watling together with Mr H.E. Thomas, J. Foster, C. Townsend, F. Fox, James Dole and G.E. Newall. Land was found at the junction of Day's Road and Kingsland Road, previously the site of a few old cottages. The building was designed by J.H. La Trobe and was officially opened in March 1888 at a cost of under £1,800. Over the years there were to be many additions and alterations to the building, which consisted of a bar and billiard room on the ground floor, two club rooms and a small room for the secretary on the first floor, together with a public hall with a seating capacity for 300 people. Above the club rooms was a second floor with a kitchen, sitting room and bedrooms for the manager or caretaker.

It provided a public house serving non-alcoholic drinks for the worker, opened at 5 a.m. to serve breakfast and closed at 11 p.m. In the evenings workers could have an evening meal, some rest and recreation.

Billiards, skittles, reading, chess, draughts, dominoes, gymnasium, cadets, brownies, boys brigade (25th), table tennis, football, cricket, swimming, cycling, brass band, male voice choir, educational classes, temperance group and the very popular Dings Club were all available here and well over 4,000 people attended each week. This place really did make a difference to the lives of local people, as this quote from around 1900 by R.W. Thompson, one of the Shaftesbury Leaders, confirms:

> It is written in the lives of men, women and children, lifted from wretchedness to joy; from squalor to comfort; from vice and neglect to happy virtue, the thrill of that first venture will not go into words; nor the early hopes, disappointments, weariness, struggle, joys and victories; nor the finding of most precious gold amid dross; nor the encounter with giants of evil, is there any place in Bristol with more happiness and laughter to the square inch than at the Shaftesbury Crusade.

After the Second World War, The Dings was listed for industrial purposes and many of the houses were demolished, but still the Crusade was to evolve. The sports club moved to Lockleaze and the building in Kingsland Road was closed, the leaders moving to the old Quaker school building in Barton Hill. It survived a fire in 1981 and is now partly restored as a charity for the homeless, but not before the old fireplaces, war memorials and the lead from the roof had been taken.

The Shaftesbury Crusade building. This picture was taken in the 1950s from Kingsland Road, looking at the Oxford Street side with its name emblazed through the middle.

The billiards room at the Shaftesbury Crusade, from a drawing by artist Samuel Joseph Loxton (1857-1922).

The Shaftesbury Crusade officers in October 1916. The three circled men are away on active service during the First World War. The picture includes members of the Tribe family; Miss Mabel Tribe is seen sitting centre front.

A children's Christmas party at the Shaftesbury Crusade, *c.* 1950.

The Dings club camp at Woolacoombe in 1906.

The Shaftesbury girls' club at Barton camp, 18-25 June 1932.

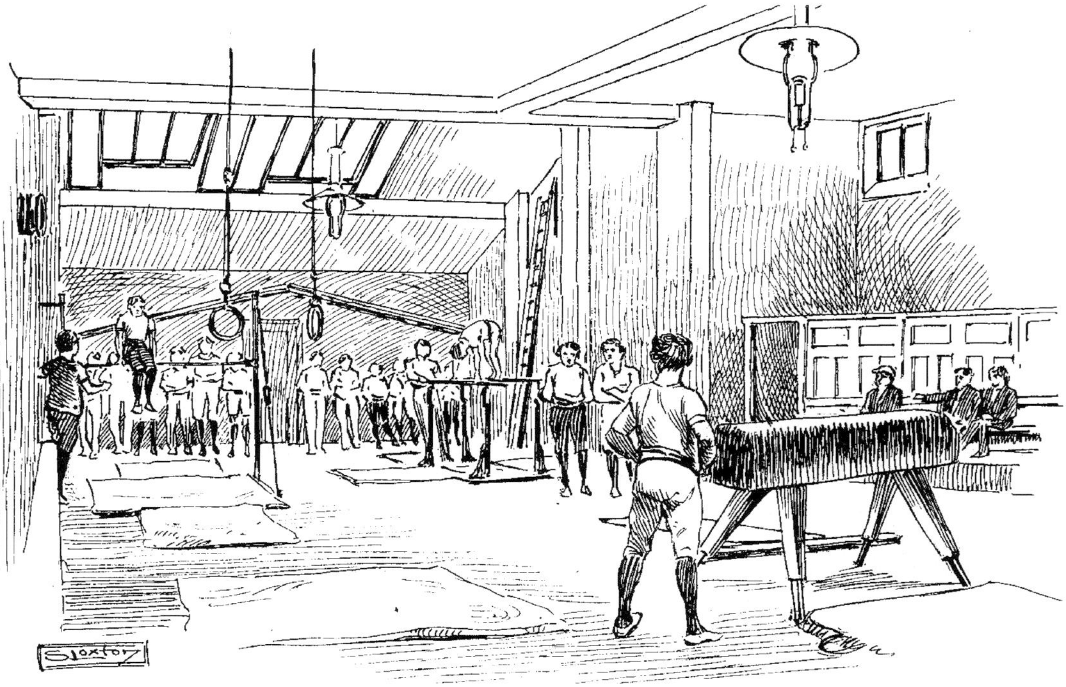

The gymnasium at the Shaftesbury Crusade, as drawn by Loxton. There were many talented youngsters in The Dings. It was the aim of the crusade to direct them into a job that used those talents.

LYNTON July 4/25

Members of the Shaftesbury Crusade in their Sunday best, on an outing to Lynton, July 1925.

The 25th Coy. Boys' Brigade, Shaftesbury Crusade, *c.* 1958. Captain Harris is making a presentation to Alfred Hunt on the occasion of his retirement as bandmaster.

Shaftesbury Crusade 'old boys' in the 1980s, founded by George Toop. From left to right, standing: Jack Harris, George Toop, Nick Patton, –?–, Harry Brooks, Gilbert Bowring. Seated: George Bullock OBE and former Sheriff of Bristol, Bill Bissix, –?–.

Left: Nurse Cox came to the Shaftesbury in 1915 and remained until at least the late 1930s. She was a well-loved lady, as was Granny Crocker, a qualified nurse who looked after the people of The Dings for over fifty-eight years before the Shaftesbury took over.

Below, left: George Toop, a man dedicated to remembering The Dings. In 1987 an exhibition called 'Yesterday's Bristol' was held at the Brunel Shed at Temple Meads station, organised by the 'yesterday's island' team, headed by Marsh boy, Brian Davies. George rallied his friends from The Dings to put together a display. It won first prize and generated a lot of interest in the district.

Below, right: Miss Mabel Tribe dedicated her life to the Shaftesbury Crusade and other local charities. The Tribe family business was Tribe, Clarke & Co., chartered accountants, auctioneers, bankruptcy and general agents based in Small Street, Bristol.

The Tribe family home, Dings House. Ernest Tribe, his wife and his sister Mabel Tribe were originally members of Redland Park church. They were instrumental in the founding of the Shaftesbury Crusade and the St Silas Mission Hall. Ernest once said 'if I have to work among the poor, I will live with them', and so he built Dings House at the junction of Union Road and Oxford Street. The family lived there until 1945, when it became the warden's house. It still stands today.

This picture really illustrates the beauty of the Shaftesbury Crusade. Note the old police box and street lamp in the left-hand corner.

Sussex Street School, *c.* 1920. Among the children is Doreen Toop (*née* Arnold) who was born in 1914. The school opened as an infant school in 1871. The children of that time took a while to get used to regular school routine and lateness was a big problem. A junior section was added in 1873. The school covered an area of 1,649 square feet and had a back entrance in an area known as the nursery. When it opened in 1871 there were just sixty-five pupils. By 1890 that had increased to 224. The school closed in 1963 and has since been demolished.

Sussex Street School annexe. Mrs Stone's class of 1957.

Mrs Dainton's class at Sussex Street School. Children seen here include: Steven Groves, Andrew Reeky, Linda Chapman, Robert Collins, Susan Davis and Trudy Blatchford.

Sussex Street School nativity play, 1955. Mary is played by Trudy Blatchford.

This drawing was taken from the original architect's designs. It shows a beautiful building, which today would probably have been listed. It was demolished in the late 1960s.

This rare photograph shows Linda Chapman, Robert Collins and Trudy Blatchford posing in front of Sussex Street School buildings, *c*. 1950.

The Dings Hammers. The local speedway team had their own track at the back of Sussex Street
School. The team's logo was two crossed hammers, and the team was run by Mr McDowell,
Jack Bryant and Harry Pitt. The team consisted of Mike Longdon, David Lewis, Ray Cavill,
Keith Stenner, John Gregory, Tony Ratcliffe, Ken Worlock, Freddy Cordy and Johnny
Holsgrove. They were Gloucestershire champions in the 1950s. Pictured are the Chilcompton
Aces (left) and Dings Hammers (right).

Left: E.H. Rowden's boot and shoe repairs, hardware and china shop, at the corner of Sussex Street and Alfred Street at No. 35. The signs read: brushes 9d and 1s 3d, mops 8d, soda 7lbs for 5d. This picture was taken around 1937.

Below: This picture shows Rowden's shop following damage in the blitz. It was repaired but lost a lot of its character.

Local children Jennifer Pitt, Trudy Blatchford, Jeannie Harvey and Elizabeth Wilson playing in the street outside The Bunch of Grapes at the junction of Alfred Street and Sussex Street, c. 1950.

Local children Jeannie Harvey, Bernice Hodge (in the pram), Trudy Blatchford and friends. In the background to the left is The Bunch of Grapes and to the right are the gasometers, c. 1950.

Visit to The Glen to see The Guinness Clock, 1951. From left to right: Yvonne Trott, Angela Bennett, Margaret Bennett, Jean Collins, Pat Long, Trudy Blatchford, Linda Chapman, Jeannie Harvey, Linda Staley, Denise Trott.

L. Harris's fish and chip shop at No. 22 Sussex Street. The business was taken over by the Swanger family who retained the Harris name. The shop was demolished in the early 1960s.

Opposite, above: The Mechanic's Arms, Sussex Street. The Ratcliffe family were for many years the licensees of this pub. Bill Ratcliffe's wife, known locally as Gran, was more than capable of removing drunken men from the premises. The Ratcliffe's were a large family involved in boxing and running several pubs in the Old Market, Barton Hill and Dings area of Bristol.

Bill Ratcliffe, known locally as Peddler, is pictured here with his brother George inside The Mechanics Arm's. The family was of gypsy origin, and once owned a large amount of land in Kingswood. Bill kept a punch bag at the Mechanic's Arms and it was here that Terry Ratcliffe learned his craft, before moving to the Apple Tree public house.

The Ratcliffe family. Terry, Tony, Peter, Patrick and Ernie (front) with their parents Sam and Topsy. Terry Ratcliffe (1930-99), won five titles in less than twelve months as an ABA Welterweight boxer before turning professional and becoming the Western Area Champion during the post-war years.

From left to right: Inch Jones, Terry Ratcliffe and Pat Patterson, long after their boxing days, meet for a reunion.

The Star, Sussex Street. Situated next to William Street, the Mechanic's Arms would have been opposite. The pub was demolished in the late 1960s.

J. Glover, grocery and provision stores at No. 115 Kingsland Road, on the corner of Oxford Street and opposite the Shaftesbury Crusade. Mr Glover traded here from around 1902-14 when these buildings were demolished. He then moved to No. 73 Kingsland Road.

King George V's Silver Jubilee party in Alfred Street, 1935. Some of the family names included in this picture are: Robbins, Whitnell, Cole, Melhuish, Brennan, Holloway, Clark, Welsh, Trickey, Purnell, Pitman, Davies, Iles, Gore, Webb, Ewans, Newman, Wilson, Nelson, Manes, Huggins, Bussell, Stone, Payne, Adams, Finch, May, Tomlins, Barman, Kelly, Ratcliffe (Mechanic's Arms), Longdon (Bunch of Grapes), Smith (who owned a grocer's shop in Sussex Street), Rowden (who owned a hardware store in Sussex Street), and a couple known as Mr and Mrs Teapot and their child 'Milk Jug'! Neighbours from Henry Street, William Street and Edward Street joined them and also relatives from Barton Hill and the Marsh.

two

From Oxford Street
to Kingsland Road

William Sheppard, from the Marsh, married Marjorie Ellen Hancock on 15 March 1933. She lived at No. 8 Oxford Street, where this picture was taken. They were both born in 1911 and had courted since they were twelve years old. They were married at St Philips and St Jacob church where both families had worshipped for generations. From left to right: Mary Sheppard (*née* Harvey), George Sheppard, the groom and his bride, William Hancock and Eva Ruby Hancock (*née* Saint). Gasometers can be seen in the background.

The Sheppards and the Hancocks in the garden of No. 8 Oxford Street, March 1933. There were no photographs outside the church and the reception was a joint effort between family and neighbours.

Right and below: St Silas Mission Hall, or St Philips Mission Hall as it was originally called, was built in around 1876 just behind the Shaftesbury Crusade. It was founded by Ernest Tribe, who built and lived in Dings House which stands opposite the hall. Inside, the building measures approximately 38ft x 60ft. It was built with a turret over the west gable and in grey pennant stone with red brick dressing. The name was changed to St Silas Mission Hall around 1900.

Four memorial stones can still be read on the front of the building. They are, from left to right, inscribed to: Mrs S.E. Marsden; Mr Eustace Brenan (who died on 12 May 1900); Master C.S.W. Horsefield; and Miss C. Riley on behalf of the subscribers of this parish. The building became St Silas Boys' Club in the 1950s, a connection with St Phillips Marsh, and later a car components factory. It has been derelict for many years.

St Silas Boys' Club annual dinner, 1951. Alderman F.C. Williams cuts the celebration cake before the meal. From left to right: R. Bryant, D. Moore, M. Radnedge, M. Saunders, R. Moore, Alderman F.C. Williams, B. Kelly, K. Randall, C. Bush, M. Davies, T. Searle.

Drawing by Loxton from around 1911, showing Kingsland Road and Gas Lane. These buildings were demolished to make way for a new workmen's club.

Above, left: A boarded-up York Street prior to demolition. A few tenants had yet to move out. There were forty-one houses on one side and thirteen on the other, with Chapel Street in between. Barton Manor estate now stands on the site. *Above, right:* Looking towards York Street, with Kingsland Road in the foreground. Kingsland Congregational church stood on the corner of this road. The shop on the left had once been a baker's shop.

Workmen pose for the camera before demolishing York Street. The demolition was completed by the early 1960s.

Barton Road. The wall to the left is part of the Jewish cemetery. Behind it was Emmanuel School. Note the cobbled streets. The road that twists around to the left is Louisa Street; this part of the road has now gone. To the right is part of the New Inn.

This photograph was taken in Sussex Street, looking across Kingsland Road towards Henry Street. On the left-hand corner was Henry Batt, tobacconist. On the right you can just see the outline of the gas tanks in Day's Road. On the right-hand corner was a shop belonging to William Parker who made ice cream. This was previously owned by Otty Wells.

This picture was taken from Louisa Street looking along Jubilee Street. Already deserted, it was soon to be demolished.

Right: The George Inn at No. 104 Kingsland Road on the junction with Day's Road, and directly opposite the Shaftesbury Crusuade. George's Place, famous for bare-knuckle fighting, was once nearby. In the 1850s The George was the venue where fighters met to arrange Sunday morning bouts. In 1982, while stripping old wallpaper, a discovery was made by landlord Graham Bell – a hidden room. Inside was Victorian memorabilia including an old pub sign. The pub closed in the 1990s.

Below: Shirley Coleman (*née* Wilson), seen here in the 1950s. She and her family lived in a flat above the Shaftesbury Crusuade, seen to the left. To the right is The George public house.

Kingsland Congregational Chapel awaiting demolition. To the left is York Street and a walk up the steps to the right would lead you to Railway Terrace and the railway bridge.

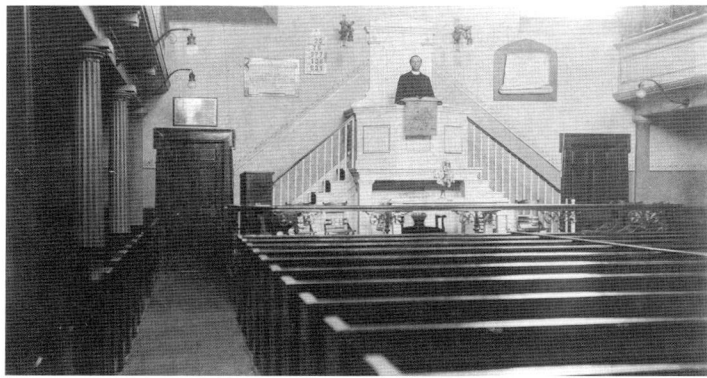

The interior of the chapel. In May 1834 Mr Frederick Wills obtained a lease of land to build this chapel. He had previously walked through St Philips on a Sunday afternoon and seen lots of children playing in the streets. He resolved to get those children into Sunday school and started in an old cottage in Sussex Street until Kingsland Chapel, named after the road in which it stood, opened on 1 December 1836.

The first leaders of the chapel were Frederick Wills, Joseph Foster, Thomas James, Mary James, Amelia Thoresbury, Thomas Crooks and Joseph Hopkins. The first sermon was preached by the Revd John Williams, known as the Martyr of Erromanga, who was in the district collecting money to fund a missionary ship to the island of Erromanga where, in 1839, he was to meet his death at the hands of cannibals. By 1888, there were 242 members and 500 children attended the Sunday school.

It was commonplace in Victorian times for wealthy churchgoers to sponsor children in the poorer parishes. One young girl from The Dings was sponsored by a lady from Woburn Sands, who sent her presents at Christmas. They arrived by railway cart, direct from the station. The building has now been demolished.

Kingsland Congregational
church Band of Hope,
5 June 1939.

Kingsland Road
Congregational church
group, c. 1930.

A very impressive display at
Kingsland Congregational
harvest festival 1922.

Kingsland Congregational Sunday School,

KINGSLAND ROAD, ST. PHILIP'S, BRISTOL.

President : Rev. T. J. MORGAN, 10 Brigstocke Road.
Superintendent : Mr. FRED. J. SNOW, 99 Ashley Down Road.
Assistant Superintendent : Mr. S. WRIGHT, "Ivydene," Montrose Avenue, Brislington.
Treasurer : Mr. W. H. HARRIS, 20 Ashgrove Road, Redland.
Secretary : Mr. A. BELSTEN, 25 Tenby Street, Lawrence Hill.

MARDONS
No 3 FACTORY.

Nov 30th 1913.

I have very much pleasure in granting
Alice Tolman a Sunday School Reference.
She has been a member of our school
since childhood & has been very regular
punctual & well behaved.
Her Teacher to whom I have referred speaks
exceedingly well of her.
She is a very respectful & respectable girl &
I can well reccommend her in full confidence

Yours truly

Fred. J. Snow

If you had a good school report and a Sunday school reference you were likely to get a job interview for one of the larger local companies like Wills, Robinsons and Mardons. This reference is dated 1913 for Mardons' no. 3 factory.

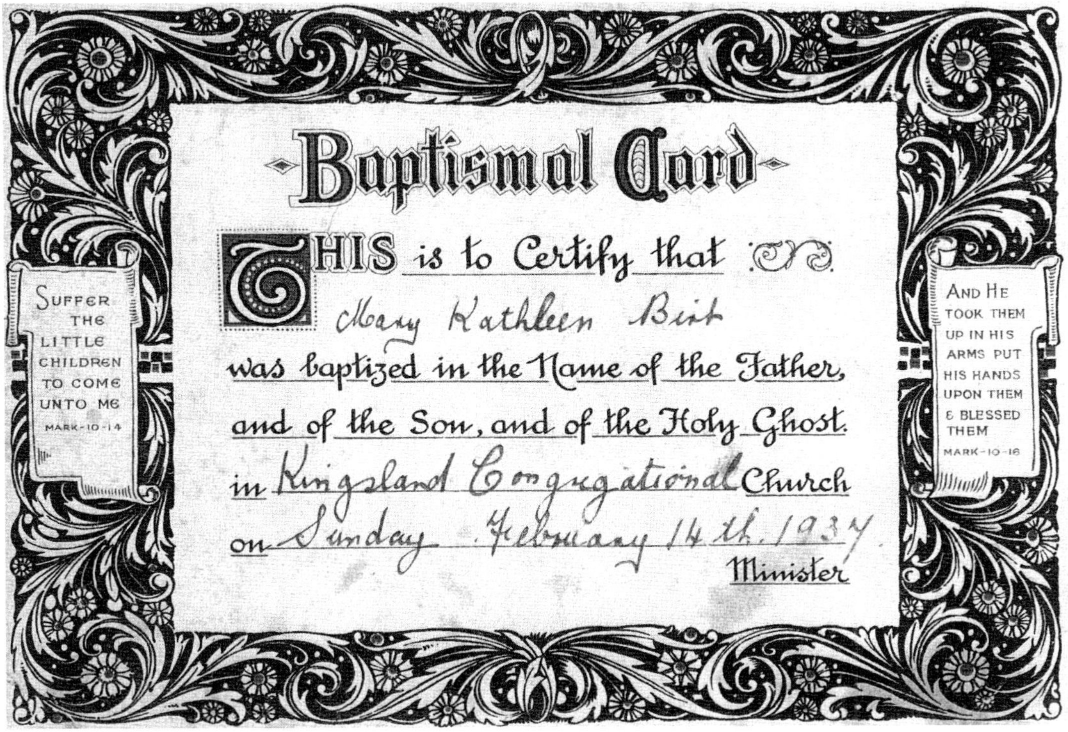

Baptismal Card

THIS is to Certify that

Mary Kathleen Birt

was baptized in the Name of the Father,

and of the Son, and of the Holy Ghost.

in Kingsland Congregational Church

on Sunday February 14th. 1937

Minister

SUFFER THE LITTLE CHILDREN TO COME UNTO ME

MARK-10-14

AND HE TOOK THEM UP IN HIS ARMS PUT HIS HANDS UPON THEM & BLESSED THEM

MARK-10-16

Above and below: Kingsland Congregational certificates.

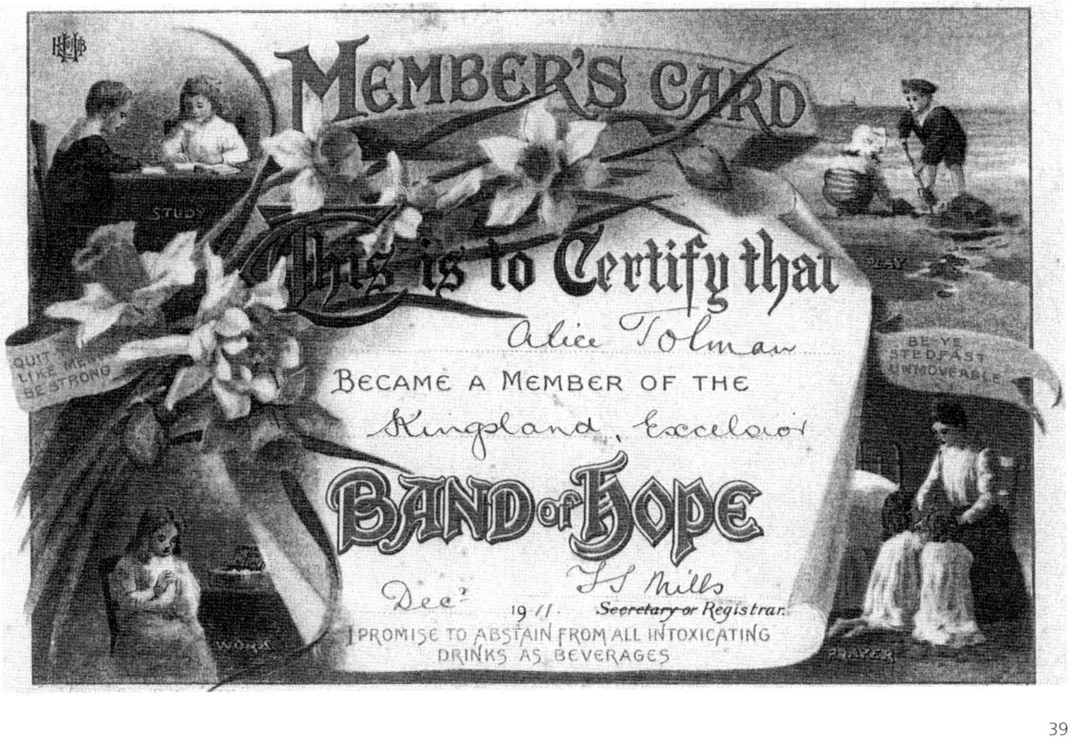

MEMBER'S CARD

This is to Certify that

Alice Tolman

BECAME A MEMBER OF THE

Kingsland, Excelsior

BAND of HOPE

T S Mills

Decr 1911. ~~Secretary or~~ Registrar.

I PROMISE TO ABSTAIN FROM ALL INTOXICATING DRINKS AS BEVERAGES

STUDY

PLAY

WORK

PRAYER

QUIT LIKE MEN BE STRONG

BE YE STEDFAST UNMOVEABLE

Left: The Victoria tavern, No. 130 Kingsland Road. To one side is the wagon works and many coal–merchants' yards, and on the other side is Queen Victoria Street.

Below: Michael and Susan Sheeley pose for a photograph near the Kingsley Road bridge, *c.* 1955. The Victoria tavern is in the background.

Opposite, above: The Berkeley Castle, No. 20 New Kingsley Road, on the corner of Russ Street (not to be confused with another Berkeley Castle public house at No. 149 Kingsland Road). Stephens Bros and Martin Ltd, who were hemp spinners, were on the opposite corner.

Bath House (beer retailer) at No. 66 Kingsland Road was situated between Sussex Street and Princess Street just a few doors away from the local Co-op store. In 1953 the premises were occupied by Mrs Kate White.

Tom Silverthorne (*left*), from Birkin Street, was killed by a tram outside The Royal Hotel on College Green in the mid-1920s. The funeral procession is seen leaving No. 118 Kingsland Road (*middle*), the address of the fish and chip shop owned by Tom's parents. The street to the left is Day's Road, and the pub on the corner is The Royal Exchange. There are at least five carriages in the procession, with many of the locals lining the street to pay their respects. The photograph was taken from the Shaftesbury Crusade. The burial was at Arno's Vale cemetery on the Bath Road (*bottom picture*).

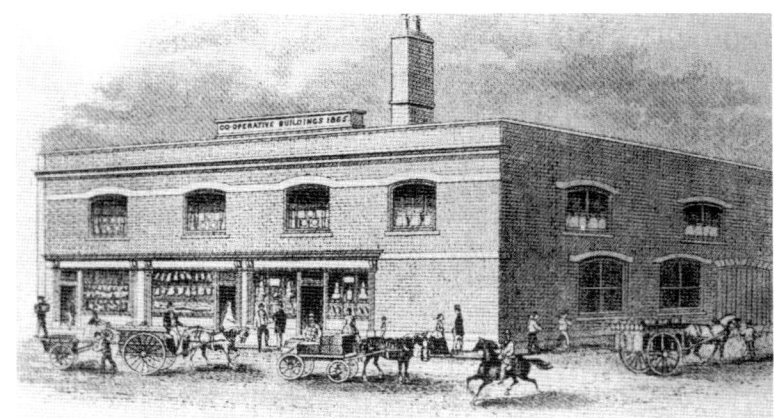

The old Kingsland Road stores, built around 1865.

The Women's Guild set up work to increase trade and membership, especially among the poorest of the neighbourhood in the early 1900s. Results were slow but successful.

WE WANT OUR MOTHERS TO JOIN THE CO OP STORE

Penny Bankers. The Women's Guild encouraged youngsters to save a penny with the Co-op. This picture was taken in Kingsland Road, *c.* 1910.

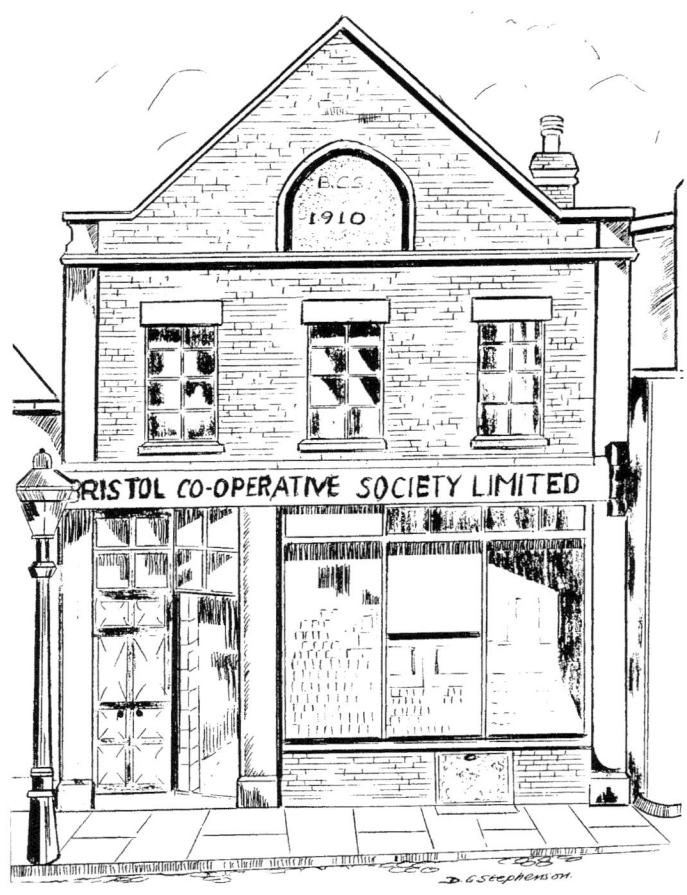

Left: The Co-op at Nos 54 and 56 Kingsland Road. The Co-op opened its first store in Kingsland Road in 1901, and this particular building dates from 1910. Situated between Sussex Street and Princess Street, the store attracted those who might be termed the 'upper crust' of the workers, chiefly railway and factory workers. Some of the poorer people shopped there but were not members: the problem for the poor was credit, they were already in debt to other shopkeepers. The store closed in the 1960s.

Below: Two advertisements for Pioneer Transport Ltd and Premier Transport Ltd, both owned by Harold Russett who lived at No. 48 Day's Road. Both companies were taken over by British Road Services, who retained the original premises.

A red-painted Pioneer Transport lorry parks outside the brick houses of Day's Road.

A Pioneer Transport lorry turning into the yard at No. 46 Day's Road. The Cumberland Street Mission is in the background.

The interior of Cumberland Street Mission. The text above the altar read 'In thy presence is the fullness of joy'. The building was situated between Nos 41 and 55 Day's Road. It was founded in 1872 by J. Hinam Bell. At the age of twenty-seven he was sent by Bristol City Mission Society to do religious work in St Philips. He was also instrumental in setting up the Shaftesbury Crusade. Cumberland Street Mission was known locally as 'Dr Bell's Mission'. Dr Bell lived at No. 22 Hayward Road, Barton Hill. He was once described by a child as dressed in a frock coat, pinstripes, black straw brimmer and wearing a monocle. There was a pipe organ in this chapel. The Mission hall was demolished in the 1960s with the money from the sale of the site going to help build a new church at Stockwood where many Dings residents were to be relocated.

Josephine Cox married Ivor Williams at Cumberland Street Mission in the late 1950s. The Cox family lived in Day's Road opposite the chapel.

Sydney Alley from a drawing by Loxton. Situated between Oxford Street and Barton Road, The Royal Mail public house was on the corner of the court in Kingsland Road. It was demolished in the 1930s as part of the slum-clearance scheme.

Another drawing by Loxton from 1911 showing a sanitised version of Hancock's Court which was next to Hammersmith Place, close to the Royal Oak and Berkeley Castle pubs on Kingsland Road. It was demolished in the late 1920s.

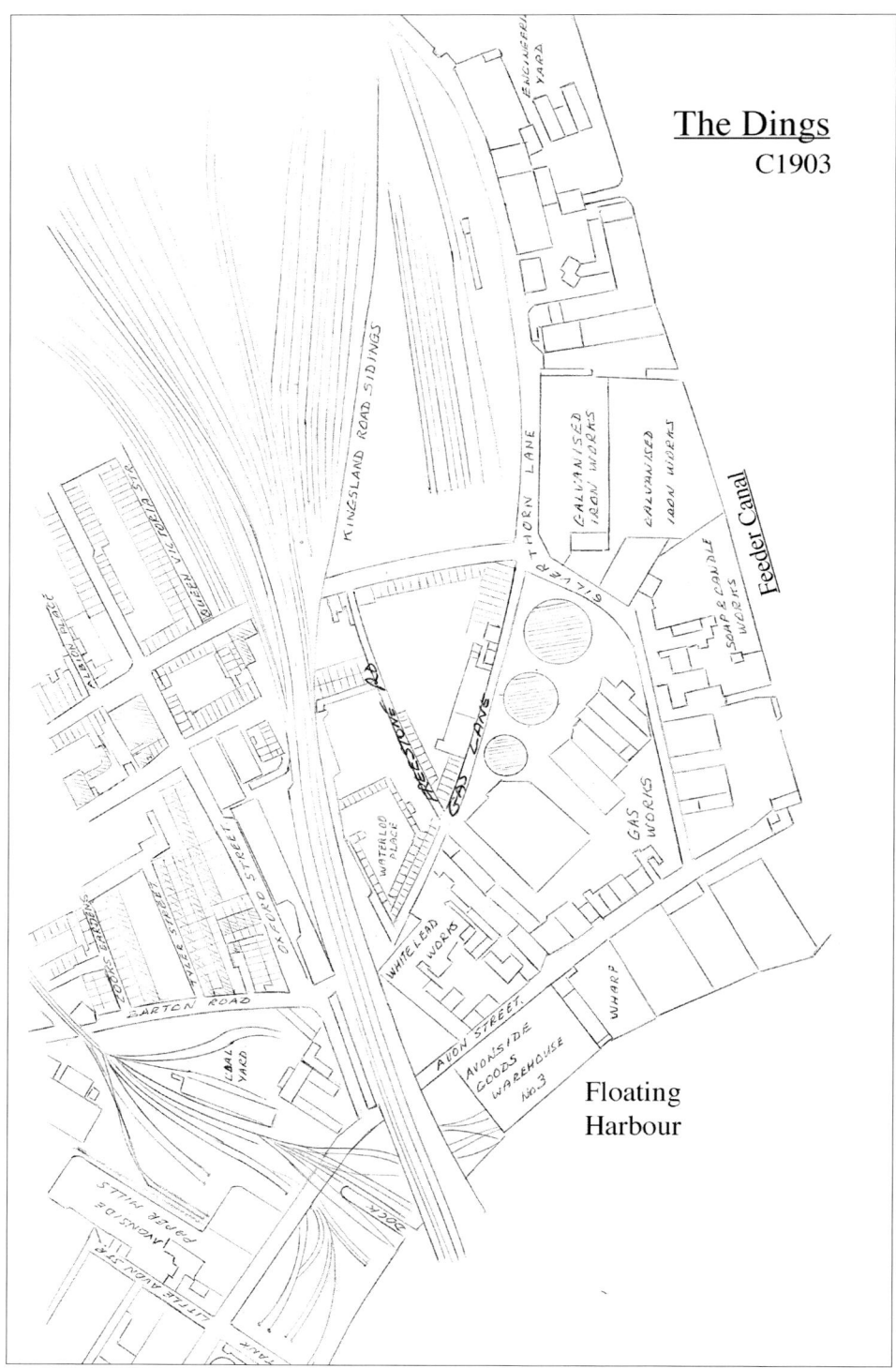

The Dings
C1903

A map of The Dings, *c.* 1903.

A map of The Dings and the Batch, *c.* 1903.

General store belonging to R. Overbury at No. 55 Barton Road. Mrs Overbury made popular home-made soups, but her specialities were pasties, brawn and pigs trotters. The shop advertises Brasso on a sign above the door and has sun guards advertising Packer's chocolates over the windows. The building is still standing but has now been converted into a house on the corner of Birkin Street.

Above, left: May Overbury sitting on the shop doorstep with the family dog. *Above, right:* Rosina and Harry Overbury in the shop doorway at No. 55 Barton Road.

The Railroad Tavern, No. 51 Barton Road. This pub was built for the Coalpit Heath railway line of the 1840s. In the picture you can see the barrier that went across the road to prevent cars and pedestrians crossing the line as a train passed through. Jimmy Brown, landlord from 1914–38, refused to serve anyone who used bad language.

The trains have long gone but part of the line and the barriers still remain.

The Duke of York, No. 39 Barton Road, was built in the 1840s on the site of an old well from which people from Union Road, Barton Vale and Barton Court drew their only source of water. In more recent years it was renamed The Barley Mow.

The residents of Tyler Street enjoy a coronation tea party in 1953.

Above: The New Inn, No. 44 Barton Road, situated on the corner of Louisa Street, close to the Jewish burial ground and opposite The Duke of York public house, owned at this time by United Beers.

Right: The New Inn, *c.* 1947. In the doorway are landlord Fred Baker (just seen on the left) with Vi and Tom Webb.

All: Barton Road cemetery. The Jewish burial ground. In 1759 this cemetery stood in the middle of the brickfields. In its earliest days the ground was leased, against Jewish law which states that a burial ground should be in eternal possession. It was finally purchased in 1859 at a cost of £210.

Today, many of the tombstones are eroded or illegible. The earliest that can be read is dated 1762 and the most recent is dated 1944. Many are written in Hebrew. There are a series of graves belonging to the Alexander family who were consuls to many European states such as Hanover, Saxony, Russia and Greece, and also the graves of Jonas Levy who was murdered in 1753, and John Braham who committed suicide in 1864.

In 1901, a fire at Mardon's factory next to the cemetery caused serious damage when firemen pulled down one of the boundary walls damaging many of the tombstones. The cemetery was restored and re-consecrated in 1903.

In 1985, a report by Benjamin Price said the cemetery was overgrown, that tombstones had been damaged and that it was being used as a rubbish dump. People took notice and it was once again restored. Today, although well hidden, it is kept neat and tidy.

This mural, commissioned by Castlemore, the developers of the Quay 2 site, has recently been painted in Avon Street at a cost of £1,000. The artist is Daniel Alias Design. The mural depicts the major changes that have taken place in The Dings since the nineteenth century.

Drawing by Loxton from around 1910 showing the Glass House Tavern at No. 38 Kingsland Road. These buildings were demolished by the 1930s. A walk up the steps would take you on to the wooden railway bridge.

On 6 November 1934 the Prince of Wales (later to become King Edward VIII) came to Bristol to see the unemployed. He had requested no flags or ceremonies. He arrived at Temple Meads station at 10.30 a.m. He visited Barton Hill and then went on to The Dings, accompanied by the Lord Mayor Alderman F.C. Luke, His Grace the Duke of Beaufort and the Chief Constable. Several houses in The Dings had been prepared for the Prince to visit, but instead he approached the home of Harry and Emily Jenkins at No. 7 Dings Walk. They were standing at their gate and he asked if he could come in. He stayed for a cup of tea and admired Harry's chrysanthemums. He then asked if he could have a bunch, which they gladly provided. Their daughter Beryl missed the event but had watched the Prince's car passing her school on the corner of Gas Lane.

three

Industry, Leisure, Education and Worship

Broad Plain Mission. In 1870 members of Highbury Chapel in Redland, under the leadership of John Linton, rented four cottages on Abbott Place in Leadhouse Lane for use as a Sunday school. These cottages provided eleven rooms and were opened for the benefit of those children whose clothes were so ragged that they could not attend any other school. This Ragged School, known as the Leadhouse Lane School, grew quickly. Within a year it had sixteen teachers with 140 children attending on a regular basis. These children were described as dirty, ragged and rude. Their clothes, such as they were, had previously belonged to their parents or older brothers and sisters. They were tied up with string and probably rarely taken off. It is reported that they had 'an odour about them.' The staff called their journey to the school from their homes in Cotham and Clifton 'the trudge'; it was obviously quite an ordeal for them.

By 1872 the premises in Leadhouse Lane had become too small and a house in Broad Plain was purchased. By now some 300 children were on the register. It is reported at this time that four boys and one girl were taken from a wretched home in St Philips and sent under care to homes in America. The school continued to grow and by 1888 the construction of a splendid new four-storey building was underway. It was opened on 13 April 1891 by Sir Joseph Dodge Weston, the local MP, and called Broad Plain House. Inspiration came from Mary Carpenter who, it is said, had 'a compassionate eye for uncared children'. In return, the Lads' Club was named the Mary Carpenter Memorial Lads' Club.

The work continued when they joined forces with the old chapel in Anvil Street. Anvil Street Chapel had opened in 1834 as a Sunday school and day school, largely under the care of members of the congregation at Highbury Chapel but, at this time, run separately from the Broad Plain Mission. The Sunday school had 550 scholars and thirty-nine teachers, eighteen of them coming from Highbury. In time, other properties in Anvil Street and Kilkenny Street were purchased and incorporated into one and by 1894 this was known as Broad Plain Lads' Club. You could enter the building from either of the two streets. The old chapel became the gymnasium. Football, billiards, cycling and camping were all organised from here. There was swimming at Broadweir Baths and the 16th Boys' Brigade Unit was set up here as well as a club for ladies.

In 1909, some of the lads expressed a desire to take up rugby and so the Broad Plain Rugby Club was born. Played originally on The Downs it was later to move to Lockleaze and Hartcliffe. The club itself, moved to purpose-built premises in Clement Street, Easton, in 1985 and the original premises were demolished in 1986.

Right: A drawing by Loxton of Broad Plain Settlement House, which opened in 1891.

Middle: Broad Plain Lads' Club, part of the Broad Plain Settlement House. The Broad Plain organisation had a presence here until the 1950s.

Below: Pictures of their successful athletic sides in various sports hang from the picture rails. A chessboard is set up on the table with snooker tables in the foreground.

Mary Carpenter Memorial Association Football Club, reserve team, 1901/02 season. From left to right, back row: J.E. Seaton (president), F. Kellard (trainer), W.H. Heskins (vice captain), W.P. Boyd, J. Edgar, F.P. Jenkins (secretary). Middle row: J. Phillips, E. Brown, W. Witcombe. Front row: C.A. Court, H. Park, F. Pike, E.C. Domaille (captain), E. Saunders.

Mary Carpenter Memorial Swimming Club Team, 1920. From left to right, back row: J.E. Seaton (vice president), W. Garmston, F.N. Colborne (president), F.J. Baker, F.P. Jenkins (secretary). Middle row: H.F. Spence, W.H. Gough, E. Ball (captain), F. Green (vice captain), A. Park. Front row: R. James, W.J. Butcher, S. Josham, E. Hobbs.

Right and below: Broad Plain Lads' Club practising gymnastics on Whitehall playing fields. Included in these pictures are Bill Bromage, Tom French, George Stone and Dick Haynes. George Stone was born in 1914 at No. 90 Kingsland Road. Two families lived in that house and George always took a dog to bed with him to keep the rats away. He attended Sussex Street School and later joined the Shaftesbury Crusade, where he discovered that he was good at gymnastics. He moved to Broad Plain Lads' Club as they had better facilities. He was also good at boxing. He later joined the army.

Broad Plain gymnastics team, *c.* 1930s.

Broad Plain Adult School, junior section, 1923. The building was opened in 1891.

THE
Broad Plain House,

ST. PHILIP'S.

DECEMBER, 1908.

THE WARDEN'S NOTES.

It is not easy for the ordinary man to realize the responsibility of citizenship in everyday home-life—he has not been trained to do so. Probably nothing, or next to nothing was taught him either by his parents at home, or by his teachers at school. It does not occur to him that he has an important part to take in the good government of the city, in its cleanliness, orderliness, and general well-being. It may be that this is the explanation of many of the wrongs and discomforts against which we are crying out to-day. We do not see that we have the remedies very largely in our own hands. The ills and neglects of generations cannot, however, be put right in a moment, but a beginning can be made. We hear much about social reforms and the need for legislation, and rightly so ; but we need not wait for legislation. We can now and here be doing something for ourselves. Character is the thing that tells, and true reformation is the renewing of the mind. This is the foundation on which all real improvement and progress are built. What a change would be wrought in a few years if every father and mother thought seriously about the future of their children, and realized their responsibilities and duties toward them. If, for instance, mothers remembered that their daughters would later on have homes of their own, and did their best to train their girls that when that time came they would know how to manage a home and keep it clean and comfortable, and how to prepare a simple meal. One does not forget the difficulties that are in the way, neither does one forget that there are many good mothers who overcome these difficulties, but proofs are not wanting that in many many homes these important matters are entirely neglected, and from childhood the girls are altogether free from control, and grow up careless and ignorant. The same kind of thing happens to the boys ; they are not taught control, or to realize the serious side of life. No matter how many Acts of Parliament are passed to better the social conditions, so long as parental responsibility and home training are disregarded, the evils of unemployment and all the consequent mischief and poverty will follow. Regular habits taught at the outset of life are absolutely necessary, and if these are neglected, the consequences must be bad. The careful home training of the children is perhaps the highest form of citizenship.

May I ask young men and women especially to think this matter over very carefully.

Warden's notes, Board Plain House, December 1908.

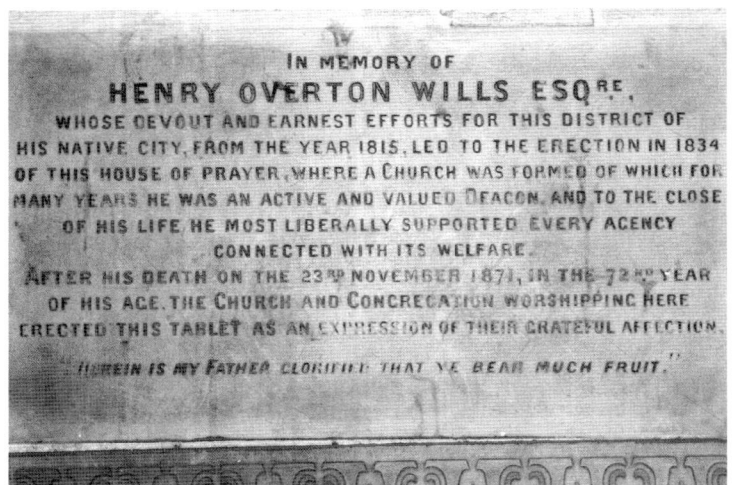

IN MEMORY OF
HENRY OVERTON WILLS ESQ^{RE}.
WHOSE DEVOUT AND EARNEST EFFORTS FOR THIS DISTRICT OF
HIS NATIVE CITY, FROM THE YEAR 1815, LED TO THE ERECTION IN 1834
OF THIS HOUSE OF PRAYER, WHERE A CHURCH WAS FORMED OF WHICH FOR
MANY YEARS HE WAS AN ACTIVE AND VALUED DEACON, AND TO THE CLOSE
OF HIS LIFE HE MOST LIBERALLY SUPPORTED EVERY AGENCY
CONNECTED WITH ITS WELFARE.
AFTER HIS DEATH ON THE 23RD NOVEMBER 1871, IN THE 72ND YEAR
OF HIS AGE, THE CHURCH AND CONGREGATION WORSHIPPING HERE
ERECTED THIS TABLET AS AN EXPRESSION OF THEIR GRATEFUL AFFECTION.
"HEREIN IS MY FATHER GLORIFIED THAT YE BEAR MUCH FRUIT."

Henry Overton Wills Esq. was a member of the tobacco family in Bristol. His activities involved the setting up of many charitable institutions in the area. The stone was destroyed when the building was demolished.

LAID BY
JOSEPH STORRS FRY
MARCH 19, 1904

Joseph Storrs Fry (1826–1913) was a devoted Quaker and pioneer in the Friends Education Movement and Sunday schools. He was a member of the Fry chocolate family and had connections to the old soap factory, being a partner of Mr Fripp.

LAID BY
P.F. SPARKE EVANS J.P.
MARCH 19, 1904.

P.F. Sparke Evans also had a park in St Philips Marsh named after him. Other stones laid in this building include those for Jonathan L. Evans, H. Arnold Thomas M.A. Stanley H. Badock and S. Day Wills JP – each one was dated 19 March 1904. Every effort was made to remove the stones on demolition but they had been too well laid.

The entrance to Broad Plain Rugby Club in Anvil Street.

Anvil Street showing the building of 1834. Inside was the gymnasium.

To the left is Anvil Street, to the right Kilkenny Street. The roof to the bottom left is the skittle alley with the glass-covered walkway leading to the snooker hall. Gardiner's building is in the background.

The snooker hall was situated on the Kilkenny Street side. The superb table was built by a craftsman.

The interior of the original chapel and school, built in 1834, which was used as a gymnasium.

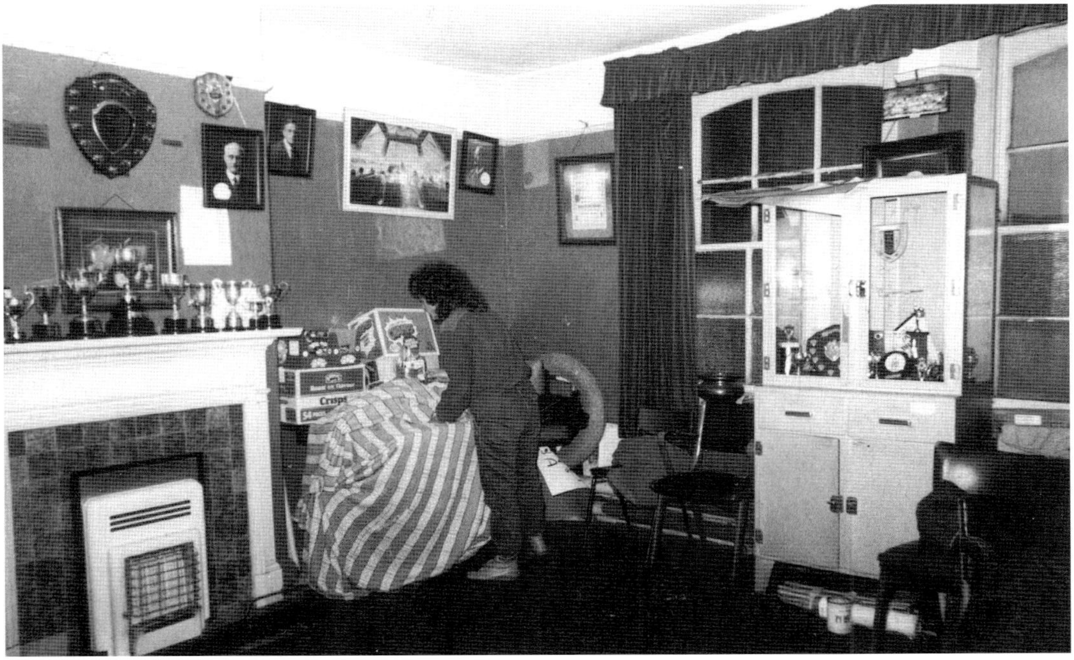

The leader's office, seen here in the 1980s. Cups, shields and photographs line the walls.

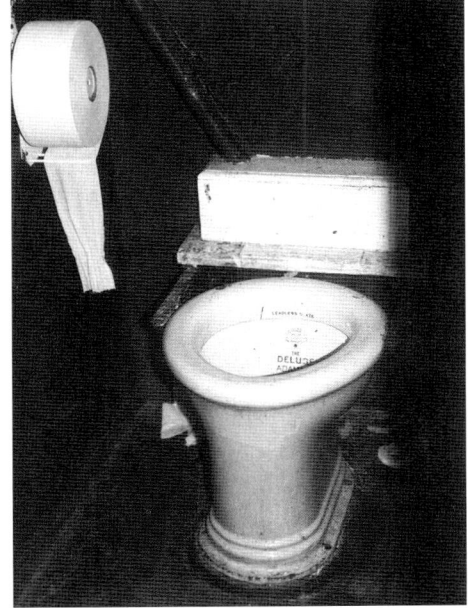

Above, left: Kilkenny Street, Broad Plain Lads' Club, later renamed the Boys' Club, was demolished in 1986.
Above, right: The ancient Deluge lavatory in the Rugby Club. The seat had been removed as a trophy by a visiting team!

Ordinary Engagements.

The following is the table for December :—

MONDAY.

2.30-4 p.m.—Mothers' Meeting.
2.30-4.—Mothers' Meeting, Anvil Street.
5.30-6.30.—Children's Hour (Girls).
6.30-7.30.—Band of Hope.
7.30-9.—Intermediate " Bee Hive " Club (Girls).
7.30-9.—Senior " Bee Hive " Club (Girls).

TUESDAY.

6.30-7.30 p.m.—Junior Boys' Swedish Drill, Anvil Street.
6-7.30.—Junior " Bee Hive " Club (Girls).
7-9.—Senior Girls' Club.
7.30-9.—Senior " Bee Hive " Club, Singing Class.
8-9.—Bible Class, conducted by the Warden.

WEDNESDAY.

2-4 p.m.—Mothers' Meeting for Mothers of S. S. Scholars.
2.30-4.—Women's Temperance Club.
6.15-7.30.—Children's Play Room.
8-9.—Christian Endeavour Society.

THURSDAY.

2.30-4 p.m.—Past Club Girls' Meeting.
6.45-8.45.—Boys' Play Room.
7-9.—Senior Girls' Club.
7.30-8.30.—Free Legal Dispensary.
8-9.—Senior " Bee Hive " Club—Physical Exercises.

FRIDAY.

6-7.15 p.m.—Children's Play Room, Anvil Street.
7-9.—" Welcome " Club (Senior Girls).
8-9.30.—Choir Practice.

SATURDAY.

7-8.30 p.m.—Branch of Penny Bank. Deposits from 1d. upwards.
Interest at the rate of 6d. in the £1 on all completed sums of 10s.
8-9.45.—Musical and Temperance Evenings, with refreshments.

ANNOUNCEMENTS.

THE HONORARY DISTRICT NURSE.

The Honorary Nurse (Miss C. M. DENSHAM), is pleased to visit anyone
needing her help or advice, at any time.
A note left at the Broad Plain House before 10 a.m., will be attended to
the same day.

THE BRISTOL FREE LEGAL DISPENSARY.

Free legal advice is given to persons unable to pay for it every Thursday
Evening from 7.30 to 8.30 o'clock, at the Broad Plain House.
J. ARTHUR H. DANIELL, LL.B., Hon. Directing Solicitor.

Above and opposite: Events at Broad Plain in 1908.

Sunday Engagements.

9 to 10.15 a.m., Men's School in Large Hall, Broad Plain.

All men are welcome, and are urged to use this opportunity for reading the Bible together and talking it over.

S. H. BADOCK, President.

2.45 p.m., Sunday School and Bible Classes, Anvil Street.

G. H. OATLEY, Superintendent.

3 p.m., Sunday School and Bible Classes, Broad Plain.

H. BRITTAN EVANS, Superintendent.

6.15 p.m., Children's Service, Broad Plain.   Miss C. MORGAN.

6.15 p.m., Children's Service, Anvil Street.   Miss CUMMINS

6.30 p.m., Service at Broad Plain House.

Subjects for the Month.			*Speaker.*
December 6. " Blessed are the Merciful "	..	..	*The Warden*
,, 13. " Blessed are the Pure in Heart "	..	..	,,
,, 20. " Blessed are the Peacemakers "	..	..	..
,, 27. " Blessed are they that have been persecuted for Righteousness sake "	..	..	,,

Communion Service last Sunday in the Month at 7.45 p.m.

8 p.m.	*ANVIL STREET.*		
December 6.	..	..	..	*Men's Morning School*
,, 13. " The Salt of the Earth "	..	..	*The Warden*
,. 20.	..	..	..	*Men's Morning School*
,, 27.	..	..	..	*Mr. J. E. Seaton*

COMING EVENTS.

December will be a very busy month. It is difficult just at present to give details ; we must pay special attention to the various notice boards and announcements. The programmes arranged for the Saturday evening entertainments are extremely good. Shall we try to do all we can to strengthen our temperance work ?

The service on Sunday evening, December 13th, will have special reference to the Girls' Clubs.

If Christmas is to be for us a season of happiness and peace, we must guard against temptations that are so commonly associated with times of festivity.

THOUGHT FOR THE MONTH.

' To get good, is animal ; to do good, is human ; to be good, is divine. The true use of a man's possessions is to help his work ; and the best end of all his work is to show what he is."

—*James Martineau.*

Opposite, above: The Crown and Anchor, at No. 13 New Kingsley Road, dated from the eighteenth century and was situated at the junction of Anvil Street and Kilkenny Street. Before the First World War the Smart family ran the pub. Mr Smart was a former glass worker so he knew most of his customers who worked at the Phoenix Glassworks. He opened the pub at 6 a.m. to serve rum and coffee. It was thirsty work in the glass factory and young lads would fetch beer in enamel pots which they suspended 'eight up' from poles to take back to the factory workers. A 1982 pub guide stated that the Crown and Anchor was 'a scrumpy pub with ageing clients and a single bar that looks into the landlord's living room and TV'.

The Crown and Anchor pub sign was quite a work of art.

The Crown and Anchor being demolished in May 2004.

John Lysaght was born in Ireland in 1832. He was educated in Bristol and acquired the business situated in Temple Back in 1857. The company employed just seven employees and made galvanised-iron buckets. The company was soon to expand, making galvanised-sheet netting, troughs, bins, tanks, cisterns and bath tubs. The site in Temple Back was becoming too small and so a four-acre site near the Feeder Canal was purchased, known as the St Vincent's Works. In 1864 the workforce numbered twenty-nine. By 1878 it had grown to 400. Trade was developed with Australia, New Zealand, Canada, South America and South Africa. During 1876, thirteen acres of land were bought at Netham, known as Feeder Farm. Here they constructed iron buildings, churches, railway stations, farm buildings, warehouses and halls. These items were sold all over the world.

John Lysaght died in 1895 aged sixty-three, but the family continued the running of the firm until 1919, when they sold their major interest to the Berry Group. It was sold again in 1920 to GKN Ltd. During the First World War things were difficult for the firm. The men were put on short time, as the zinc they needed for production came from Belgium which was occupied by the German army. The general strike of 1926 also had a devastating effect on production and during the Second World War the St Vincent's Works were singled out as a target for German bombers. During this time the company was making bailey bridges and involved in the construction of a petrol pipeline linking England to France after the D-Day landings. The Netham Works at this time were producing amphibian crafts and anti-submarine netting, anti-aircraft guns and shells, much of this work being carried out by women.

In 1950 Rheemco Lysaght was formed to make oil drums at the St Vincent's Works. 1970 saw the close of the Netham Works and the buildings were demolished in 1976. Rheemco Lysaght became Rheemco Ltd and then Blagden Packaging before they moved to Avonmouth in 1995. The St Vincent's Works were purchased by Garrad Hassan in August 2000. Since then, there has been much refurbishment including the removal of a lot of so-called modernisation to emphasise this as one of Bristol's most beautiful buildings. It is opened to the public once a year and is well worth a visit.

Advertisement for John Lysaght Ltd from the Professional and Trades Directory, *c.* 1928.

St Vincent's Works, Silverthorne Lane, built from locally quarried pennant stone. It was designed by Thomas Lysaght, the brother of John, but the work was carried out by another architect, R. Milverton-Drake, whose name and the date 1891 are carved into the stone above the door.

The City of Bristol coat of arms forms a central part of the mosaic floor in the entrance hall of St Vincent's Works.

This picture shows the breathtaking interior of the building, which includes a linked staircase and octagonal hall surrounded by offices. The walls are decorated with Royal Doulton tiles in a variety of designs, all made especially for this building. Around the domed ceiling is a frieze of golden boats on a green background.

Two photographs of the interior, showing the impressive tiling.

POWELL & RICKETTS,
Phœnix Glass Bottle Works,
ST. PHILIP'S, BRISTOL.

Above and below: The Bottle Works. Benjamin Lund, who was a brass founder and stay maker, started the works here. It later became part of Hooper's Glassworks. In 1750, Messrs Wadham, Ricketts & Co. bought what was known as the Phoenix Glassworks and by 1789 it had been converted into a glass bottle manufacturer. Later it was to become Powell & Ricketts, The Phoenix Glass Bottle Works. It closed in 1923.

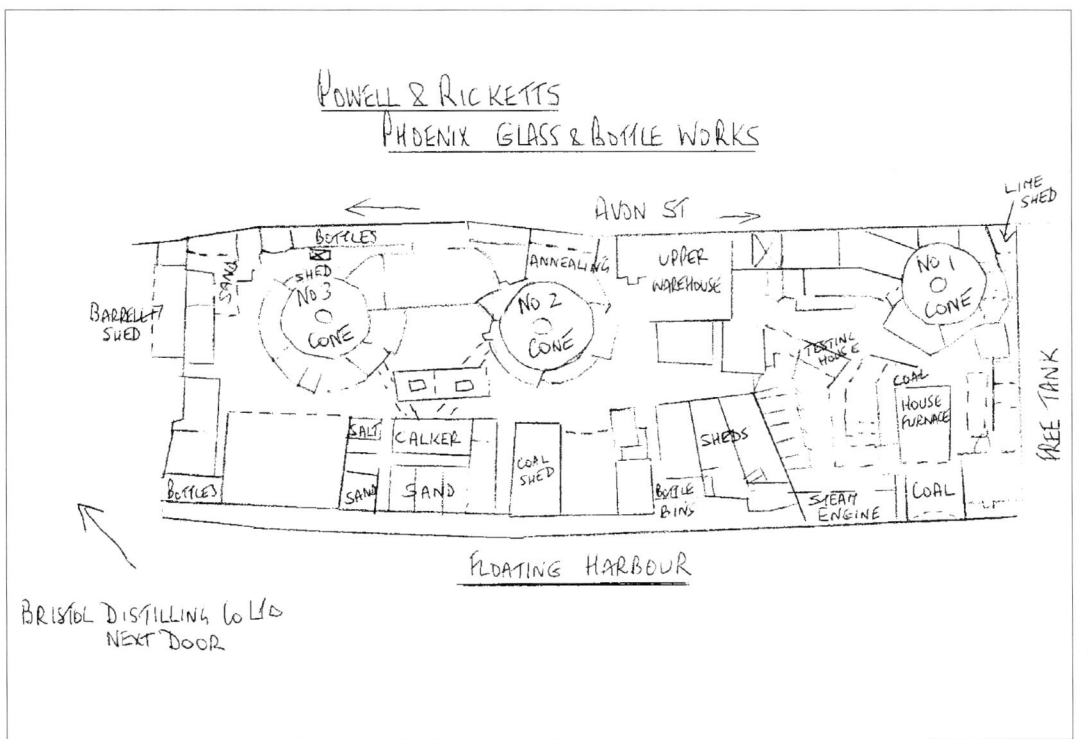

Eddie Hapgood, Bristol's greatest footballer. Edris Albert Hapgood (Eddie) was born on 24 September 1908 at Clarke's Buildings, Union Road, St Philips, which stood next to St Silas Mission Hall. He was the second youngest in a family of six girls and four boys, and went to Emmanuel School.

In 1914, the family moved to nearby No. 23 Ranelagh Street, Barton Hill. It was here that he was fined 2s 6d for playing football in the street and breaking a window. After his time at Emmanuel School he attended Hannah More School which was situated in Trinity Road.

He had a trial for Bristol Rovers after they saw him playing on The Downs for St Philips Adult School. Rovers offered him a contract but he signed a better deal with Kettering. Here, he was spotted by the legendary Arsenal manager Herbert Chapman and was signed for £750.

Considered to be of slight build, he was given steak to build him up. He made his debut for Arsenal on 19 November 1929 and he would go on to make 434 league and cup appearances for them, many of them as captain. Between 1930 and 1938 they won five league titles and reached three Wembley FA Cup Finals. His first international match for England was in May 1933 when he played in Rome against Italy. Legend has it that in making a clearance, Eddie kicked the ball into the crowd, hitting Mussolini.

One year later he was captain of England, again playing against Italy, who turned in a very dirty game injuring many of the England players including Eddie, who had his nose broken. He continued to play, however, and England won 3-2.

In 1938 England played Germany in Berlin in front of a crowd of 110,000. The team were instructed to give the Nazi salute. They objected but were forced to do so by team officials. They went on to win the match 6-3. Eddie played a record forty-three times for England and was captain on thirty-four occasions. The war was to bring his career to a premature end. He served in the RAF where he still managed to play football. He retired in December 1945 holding the record for the most caps for his country. He later became manager of several smaller clubs including Bath City from 1950-56.

Eddie died on 20 April 1973 aged sixty-four, but will always be remembered as 'the prince of the fullbacks'; technically exceptional, never a better tackler, with a sound positional sense which allowed him to not only cut off passes intended for wingers but also cover his centre half. He was elegant, polished, unruffled and calm. Eddie was rightly selected by the Football League in their Hall of Fame as one of the best 100 league players of all time.

Winston Churchill greets the England team before a match with Scotland at Wembley in October 1941.

Eddie Hapgood introduces his team to King George VI at Wembley. Here, at the age of thirty-four, he had played forty-three times for England.

This plaque was erected by the Barton Hill History Group on 24 September 2003 in memory of Bristol's greatest footballer Eddie Hapgood. It is situated in the wall of the former Adult School in Salisbury Street, Barton Hill. Mike Hapgood, Eddie's son, had the honour of unveiling the plaque, along with former Bristol City player Paul Cheesley and former Bristol Rovers player Alfie Biggs.

The Bristol Gas Light Co. was formed in 1815. They built their first gasometer near Templeback. Within a few years the demand grew and the Avon Street site was purchased. The foundation stone was laid on 6 March 1821, with many coins being deposited under the stone to mark the occasion.

Much of the coal used in this process arrived by cart or by barge and as the demand grew over the next few years, many other plants were built around Bristol. The company also purchased land in Day's Road with the railway lines leading to Barrow Road train sheds and Folly Lane behind them, about half a mile away from the gas works itself. Here they built two gasometers. The first was erected in 1873; it was 80ft tall and held 1,500,000 cubic feet of gas. The second was built in 1894; it was 150ft tall and held 5,000,000 cubic feet of gas. The smaller of the two was in use until 1976. Both were demolished in 1981. The gasometers rose and fell according to consumption. In 1949 the industry was nationalized and became British Gas.

The Bristol Gas Light Co. buildings in Avon Street, from a drawing by Loxton. On top of the building was a weathervane featuring a man carrying a ladder.

Local hero George Daniel Jones (1900-1969). Born in 1900, George served in the First World War, while underage, and saw action in France and Germany. When he returned home he found, like many others, that there were few jobs and he remained unemployed until 1926 when he obtained a job with the Bristol Gas Light Co. He married Lily and they lived in a cottage at No. 24 Folly Lane, a company house within a few feet of the largest gas holder in the West Country.

Sport was George's passion. He had played football for St Philips Adult School (known as Freestone School), The Union Jacks, City and Rovers as an amateur, had trials for Chelsea and won county caps for Gloucestershire in 1927 and 1928. He was also a great swimmer. With a small group of lads from Broad Plain Boys' Club, he formed The Bristol Central Swimming Club in January 1927. He was also the local swimming correspondent for the Bristol *Green 'Un*.

Then the Second World War came. The first major attack on Bristol started with a siren warning at 6.21 p.m. on Sunday 24 November 1940 and by 7 p.m. incendiary bombs were being reported in the St Philips area. Two of these became lodged on top of the gas holder in Day's Road. Without hesitation, George took his respirator and steel helmet and climbed the 80ft to the top. Since he needed both hands on the ladder, he took no other equipment. At the top, he steadied himself on the rail which ran around the top. He kicked one incendiary over the edge, breaking his toe in the process, he then scooped another incendiary with his helmet, throwing it over the side into water below. During the same raid the holder was punctured several times by bomb splinters and flying shrapnel. George managed to plug each hole with clay. If he had been unsuccessful in his efforts, Barton Hill and The Dings would probably have changed long before the City Planner did the job.

George was in action once again on 11 December 1940, when one of the gas holders was badly punctured and set alight. George, although off duty, bravely fought the fire, together with other employees, extinguishing it and stopping the escaping gas.

On May 2nd 1941, it was announced that George Jones had been awarded The George Medal, which was duly presented to him at Buckingham Palace.

In 1948 he was appointed coach and scout for Britain's Olympic Swimming Team. Many of his swimmers won national titles and reached the Olympic and Commonwealth Games. He was also involved in swimming for the disabled. Although regarded as a professional coach he rarely took any payment for his services. He died suddenly on 24 February 1969.

ON THIS SITE DURING AN ENEMY AIR RAID ON 24 NOVEMBER 1940
GEORGE DANIEL JONES OF FOLLY LANE
PREVENTED A MAJOR DISASTER
BY REMOVING INCENDIARY BOMBS FROM BRISTOL'S LARGEST
GASOMETER FOR WHICH HE WAS AWARDED THE GEORGE MEDAL

BRISTOL
DEVELOPMENT
CORPORATION

British Gas

This plaque commemorating George Jones' bravery was erected in 1995 at a spot in Day's Road, near to where the gas holders once stood. His son and daughter were present at the unveiling. Dings historian Benjamin Price had campaigned for years for a plaque in George's honour.

Bristol

2 Gasanstalten der Bristol Gas Company
Länge (westl. Greenw.) 2° 34' 30" Breite 51° 26' 55"
Missweisung: -12° 46' (Mitte 1939)

1:63 360 Bl. Nr. 111
1:100 000 Bl. Nr. 32

Koksofenbatterie
Gasreinigung u. Gewinnung v. Nebenprodukt.
Gasbehälter.

Maßstab 1:10 560

Stand Sept. 193

German map used by the Luftwaffe during the Second World War. Dated 1939, the gas works at Day's Road and Gas Lane are clearly marked as targets.

Opposite, below: Gas Lane from a drawing by Loxton. The children have no shoes; a common site in The Dings. In time they would receive boots from the Lord Mayor's fund. Cottages, now long gone, can be seen looking toward Lysaght's with the gas tanks to the right of the picture.

Second World War Fire Incidents in St Philips. These are a few of the more serious incidents:

---

25 June 1940: Fire at Unity Street, Barleyfields School, goods yard, Midland Road, Soap Works, Broad Street, Avonside Paper Mills, Jacob Street and Old Market.

24 November 1940: Sussex Street, LMS goods shed, Avon Street, Butler's, Union Road, Kingsland Road, Old Market tram wires down, gas holders, Day's Road.

2 and 3 December 1940: Old Bread Street, United Yeast Co. in Cheese Lane, Thomas's soap factory, Avon Street, house opposite St John Ambulance, Unity Street.

6 and 7 December 1940: LMS train in St Philips station. Avon Street, Cheese Lane, Barton Road and Oxford Street, distillery, Upper Cheese Lane, almshouses in Old Market, Pickfords in Avon Street, plus several fatalities.

11 December 1940: Bristol Gas Co., Day's Road (*see* George Jones story), York Street.

3 and 4 January 1941: Thomas's soap factory, Barleyfields School, Smith, Stone & Knight, Avon Street, Warriner's food store, Midland Road, Central Health Clinic, Tower Hill, Cole and Potlow tailors, West Street, Thomas Rowcliffe & Sons, Waterloo Road, The Drill Hall and Kear's Engineering Store, Butler's, Silverthorne Lane, Spear Bros & Clarke Ltd, Broad Plain, Hurwood's pram shop, Old Market.

16 and 17 March 1941: Thomas's soap factory, Broad Plain, Olympia cinema, Careys Lane, Simmonds brewery, Jacob Street, Taylor's, David Street, Distillery, Avon Street, Flax Mills, New Kingsley Road, Three Horseshoes, Old Market, Lyon's, Redcross Street.

7 and 8 May 1941: Flax Mills, New Thomas Street; Cooperage, Kingsley Road; Smith, Stone & Knight, New Kingsley Road; Thomas's soap factory, Simmonds Brewery; Cabinet Works, Barton Road.

The electricity generating station on Feeder Road received a direct hit to the switch-gear room and supply was cut to a number of factories engaged in war work.

Right: George Sheppard (seated) ran a shop on Feeder Road and also rented the stables to the side of The Rising Sun. He and Bill Jefferies (standing), the landlord of The Rising Sun, were very good friends. The Sheppard family continued to run the shop in Feeder Road until the 1980s.

Below: The Rising Sun, Avon Street, situated between Cheese Lane and the Feeder Canal. Gypsies often traded horses in the yard or sold Gypsy 'gold' rings to the locals. The pub was demolished in the 1960s.

Len Munden started out as a boxer. In 1939 he was the Western Lightweight Champion and was rated fifth in Britain. He had ninety-three fights, of which he lost only fourteen. Then tragedy struck. While serving in the RAF during the Second World War Len lost his left arm, which ended his boxing career. But he didn't give up. After six years fighting red tape he was to become the only one-armed PSV/bus/coach driver in the country. Losing his left arm was a huge problem as a driver, the gear stick being on the left side, but he found a way to put his right arm through the steering wheel to change gear. The school children riding his bus would watch in amazement!

Above and below: Len Munden, Crown Coaches, Freestone Road. During the business' early years Len would only purchase Leyland vehicles. JYD 95 (above) is a 1948 Leyland Tiger half cab. It was painted red with a cream roof and stripe along the side. Len later acquired Empress and Monarch Coaches. The business is now run by his son.

The railway arch between Freestone Road and Oxford Street still stands today. It was very well used by school children going to St Philips Board School in Freestone Road.

In 1873 The British Board Schools advertised for tenders to build Bristol's first Board School. It opened in August 1874. Officially called St Philips Board School, it was known locally as Freestone Road School because of its two entrances: one in Freestone Road and the other in Gas Lane.

Designed by Stuart Colman and redesigned in 1897 by F. Bligh Bond it covered an area of 1,335 square yards. Unfortunately, no drawings or photographs of the building itself have been found, but according to Walter Leither, who was born nearby, it was five stories high, and built with old red bricks with ornate turrets on the top. It had wobbly stairs and the floors were made of pine. In 1882, according to the school log book, the accommodation was full with 190 children in attendance. Children who travelled in caravans with their parents attended this school. It is mentioned in the log book when they left, 'Caravan people left district'. They had come previously from South Wales.

On 4 July 1922 The Lord Mayor and Lady Mayoress paid a visit to the school. It opened originally as a boys school, adding infants in 1924 and junior mixed in 1936. The pupils were moved to Sussex Street during the Second World War because of the possibilities of daytime raids.

The school closed in 1963. SWEB used it for a short time, until the building was demolished.

Freestone School, c. 1926. Some of the girls pictured include Mabel Thorn (her father kept a shop in Kingsley Road), Nellie Williams, Lily Gunter, Margaret Fisher, Edna Chilcott (who lived in Edward Street), Phyllis Wheeler, Louise Ackerman, Doreen Arnold (centre, with glasses and pinafore). The teachers are Miss Tibbett (right) and Miss Gracie (head teacher, back left).

Freestone School, c. 1927. Rosina Hewitt (seen here in the second row, third from the left) attended Sussex Street School until she was seven, before moving to Freestone School. She is believed to be aged around seven or eight in this picture. Some of the girls are wearing red ribbons on their pinafores, believed to be given as a prize for good work.

Bristol Education Committee.

St. Philip's Girls' SCHOOL.

Certificate of Character.

Name of Child .... Doreen Arnold ....

Date of Birth .... 19. 9. 14 ....

Address .... 13 William St. St. Philip's ....

Standard, or corresponding class, in which the child was working at time of leaving school .... Std 9 ....

Time spent in above-named school .... 3 yrs. 9 months ....

Regularity .... Absent 4 days during past year .

Punctuality .... Late twice   „   „   „

Diligence .... Excellent

Conduct .... Excellent

Remarks (if any) .... Doreen is an all-round, bright, intelligent girl. She is clean, industrious and trustworthy. She has excelled at her school work and is one of the 3 top girls of the school.

Signature of Head Teacher .... E. W. Heard.

Date .... Oct. 25th 1928.

W.B.—10m/8/24   No. 20A

Certificate of Character, St Philips Girls' School, Freestone Road. Doreen Arnold was considered to be one of the top three girls at her school. With this certificate and another from the church she attended, she secured an interview for a job at Wills and was taken on.

William Street coronation tea party, 1937. There were thirty-six houses in this street with front doors opening directly onto the pavement. William Street ran between Princess Street and Sussex Street.

Alfred Street coronation tea party, 1937. The street, containing thirty-one houses and The Bunch of Grapes public house, ran between Sussex Street and Princess Street.

Above left: Union Road, *c.* 1921. Stanley Wheaton is here somewhere. The fold of the picture goes through Fred Griffiths. To his right is Albert Griffiths. Next to him, with the white hair, is Tom Croot. Miss Badman, who made the little pinafores that the girls wore to school, is also here somewhere. Williams and Hewitt also appear in the picture. They lived at Nos 45 and 52 Union Road. To the left of the picture is Cottage Place, demolished in 1936. The following piece was written by William Gregor, from The Dings, in the 1920s:

Cottage Place contained about six cottages around a closed court which was entered through a passage set into one side. No electricity, gas or running water, just a well with a tap at the entrance of the courtyard. It contained a sink, which was salt glazed and built into two courses of bricks. Every morning, men would line up to wash, some stripped to the waist, others with sleeves rolled up and the necks of their shirts tucked in.

The cottages were one up and one down (hovels) with back addition wash house containing a boiler in the corner for the weekly wash. The rent was 3/6 a week. Roofs leaked. Buckets were placed where the water came through. The roofs sagged in the middle. They would have collapsed if any repairs were attempted. They never were.

The front door opened into the living room, as did the back. You had to be careful when shutting the door or windowpanes would fall out. The toilet was in the yard. Everyone shared it. No flush, just a hole, bricked up with a board running the width of the toilet, with a hole cut in the middle. Rats often climbed out, as a few unlucky people could testify!

Above right: Coins Buildings, Union Road, in the 1920s, showing Ivy Pippins, the Woodford family and William Gregor, fourth from the left aged about seven. Note the condition of the houses with the roof already in danger of collapse.

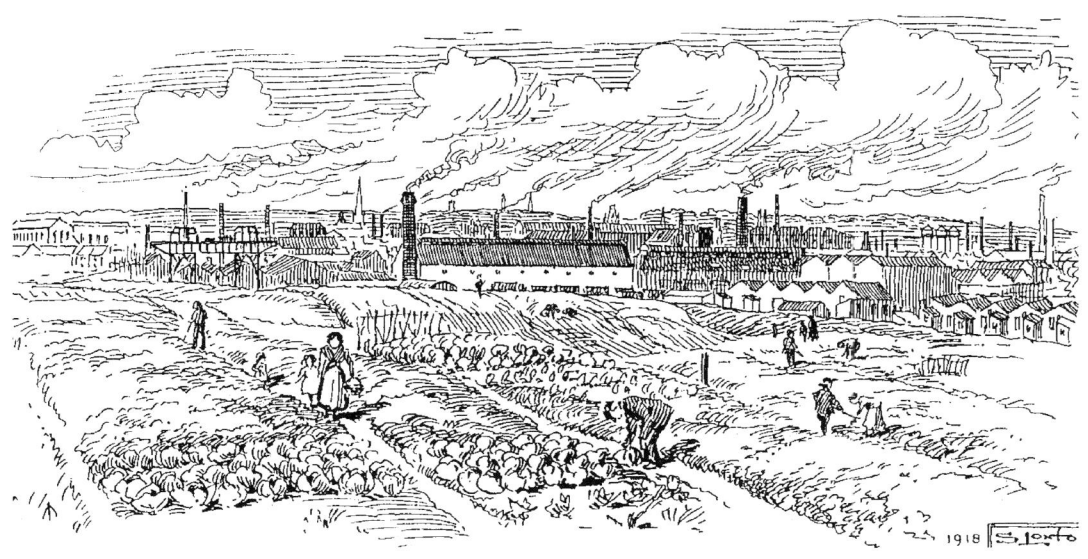

Barton Place, seen here around 1910, was one of many small courts off Union Road.

Drawing by Loxton, *c.* 1918. St Philips Marsh looking towards The Dings, showing market gardens and allotments. Most working-class people grew their own produce if they could.

Inch Jones (Henry) was born at No. 56 Grafton Street in St Philips Marsh in 1909. He took the name Inch from his uncle, and they became known as Little Inch and Large Inch. To earn extra money he often boxed in the booths at the local showgrounds around The Batch and in places around Old Market. A featherweight, known as 'a knockout specialist from St Philips' and described as debonair, he took a pride in his clothes and was even asked to model clothes for the 50/- tailors. He was later to work at St Ann's Board Mills as a welder. He died in 1978.

Barleyfields School, New Kingsley Road. The school was opened in 1891 in Horton Road, between the Batch and Upper Cheese Lane. It was designed by F. Bligh Bond, the architect of many of Bristol's Board Schools as well as St Aidan's church, Nags Head Hill, St George Technical School and Cossham Hospital. The school covered an area of 6,308 square feet.

Class photograph from around 1970, with teacher Pat Jones, an ex-pupil of Colston School and daughter of local hero George Jones.

Class photograph, Barleyfields School. Taken in the late 1920s.

Class 3A from Barleyfields School, June 1936. Hilda Arnold is one of the girls holding the board.

Barleyfields School, 1938/39 season. In the picture are Joey Ratcliffe (from the boxing family), Ernie Peacock (captain) known as Ginger Peacock. He went on to play thirteen seasons at Ashton Gate for Bristol City, making 357 appearances. He later moved to Weymouth. He died in 1973 aged forty-eight.

Emmanuel church, on the corner of Midland Road and Kingsland Road. From the outset the building of this church was difficult. Twenty-seven-foot deep foundations had to be dug as the ground was so marshy. The foundation stone was laid on 21 August 1860 and the church opened on 9 December 1862. It was constructed from Hanham stone with freestone dressings and Bridgwater tiles. It seated 700 people of which 400 were free. There was no tower but a double bellcote over the chancel arch.

The first vicar was the Revd Cornall who stayed for forty years. He started a ragged school in nearby Sidney Alley and also raised the money to start the Emmanuel School in Louisa Street in 1883 catering for 450 children. Eddie Hapgood, the Arsenal and England footballer, was a pupil at this school. Emmanuel School amalgamated with Freestone School in 1947.

In March 1899, William House, a haulier, of No. 62 York Street, was sweeping out the church when he made a tragic discovery; the body of a newborn child wrapped in a brown paper parcel. An inquest stated that it had died from want of attention at birth.

The church closed in 1937 due to subsidence. A supporting pillar had been built too close to the Wainbrook which ran underneath the church. When it came to demolishing it in 1938, the contractor simply tied ropes and chains around the pillar and pulled. With little effort the building collapsed.

The interior of Emmanuel church, *c.* 1927.

The wedding of Winifred Durston of York Street and Herbert Nicholls of Waterloo Street at Emmanuel church in 1927. The baby held in the back row is Delphine Rowden. The vicar was Henry Hill and the photographer P.M. Mower, of No. 23 Clarence Road.

Emmanuel church had its own scout group; the 19th Bristol.

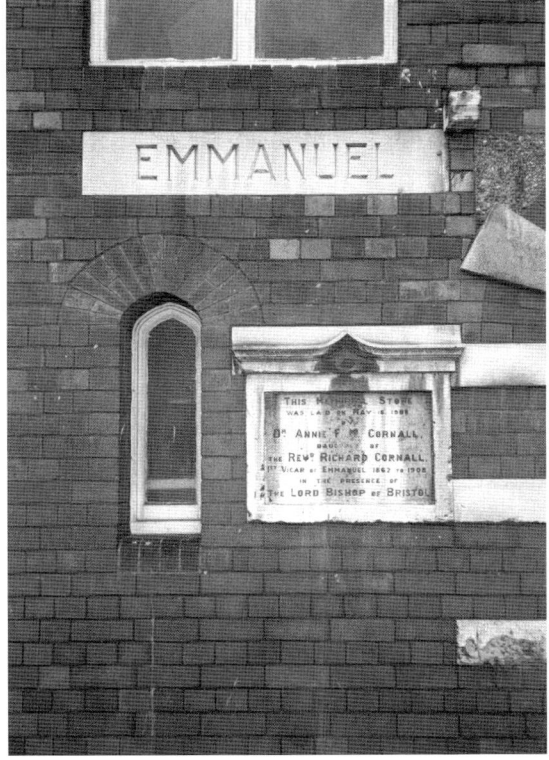

Above: Emmanuel Hall is today still standing but is currently in between uses .

Right: The stone memorial on the front of Emmanuel Hall reads: This memorial stone was laid on 16 May 1908 by Dr Annie F.M. Cornall, daughter of the Revd Richard Cornall, the first vicar of Emmanuel (1862-1908) in the presence of The Lord Bishop of Bristol.

Snooker at Emmanuel Hall, *c.* 1951. From left to right, at the front, are: Keith Caddick, Tony Stallard, Terry Hall, John Watts, Lord Mayor Norman Saga and Jack Brooks.

Emmanuel Hall, early 1950s. The lady to the left is Lily Savage, Sunday school teacher, Tony Stallard is to the right wearing glasses. Also pictured are: Mike Griffith, Graham Light, Barry Coombs and Arthur and Hilda Dale and their children.

Christmas party at Emmanuel Hall, early 1950s. In the group are Tony Stallard, the Dale family, M. Griffith, Graham Light, Lily Savage, Diane and Ann Hooper, and Barry Coombs.

Emmanuel School, 1937/38. From left to right, back row: Mr Ware (headmaster), Douglas Buckingham, Graham Gore, John Hoskins, John Barman, 'Tricky' Davis, Peter Drew, Ron Martin, Jack Chaplin, Mr Barratt (teacher). Second row: Delphine Rowden, Grace Plumley, Edna Pratt, Joyce Richards, Joan Ford, -?-, Lily Coles, Lily Connell, Eileen Blanin. Front row: names not known.

Emmanuel School, 1937. Those seen here include: Royston Lovell, Peter Drew, Mr Ware (headmaster), John Jones (later became a swimming champion), Jack Chaplin, Graham Gore, John Barman, Grace Plumley, Delphine Rowden, Eileen Blanin, Bessie Turner, Leslie Brown, Roy Dursley, Albert Brooks, Royston Davidge, Joan Taunton, Doreen Stephens, Doris Spiller, Joyce Cox.

Above and below: Habgood & Co. situated at the junction of Gas Lane and Freestone Road. Take a look at this building carefully. Would you believe that it was formerly the United Methodist Free church? Take away the front porch and perhaps it becomes a little more obvious but the only real clues are inside (which was once timbered, and had its own organ). The bricked–up outlines of the arched windows remain. The United Methodist Free church was opened in 1859 near an area known as Tyler Field. It closed in 1927 and became a flour warehouse. Local people remember seeing the 'feathery flake' sign outside. A lift was added to take the flour bags to the new second-floor level. Later it became the Victoria Flour Co., which eventually moved to Avonmouth. Habgood's started out in 1832, their original premises being at No. 42 Castle Street where they stayed until the blitz. They then moved to Oxford Street before taking over these premises around 1990.

Telegrams : "HABGOOD BROTHERS, Bristol."   Established 1832.
Telephone : 760, Bristol.

HABGOOD BROTHERS,

Cash Buyers
of
Scrap Iron,
Steel,
Metal,
Metal Residues,
Rubber,
etc.

CASTLE GREEN,

BRISTOL.

MANUFACTURERS of Ingot Brass, Type, Spelter, Solder, etc.

Right: Although closely linked with Kingswood and Hanham Mount, a world Methodist Heritage Site, John Wesley gave his first open-air sermon on 2 April 1739 at a site known as Brickfields, St Philips. This plaque was erected close to the site to commemorate the historic event.

Below: An aerial view showing the Feeder Canal flowing into the floating harbour. Cross the bridge from the Marsh and the first building on the right is The Rising Sun. Opposite that is what was known as the coke house. Avon Street is the first road that leads to the gas works. Its tank can be seen at the top of the photograph. Running through the middle is Silverthorne Lane which leads to Lysaght's steelworks.

NEAR THIS PLACE
ON APRIL 2nd 1739

JOHN WESLEY

PREACHED IN THE OPEN AIR
FOR THE FIRST TIME
IN THIS COUNTRY

ISAIAH 61:1
LUKE 4: 18—19

Spear Bros & Clark Ltd was started by George Edwin Spear in 1875, who was joined soon afterwards by his bothers Fred and Edward as the business expanded. The bothers later acquired the firm of William Clark & Sons, who traded in Victoria Street, and the name changed to Spear Bros & Clark Ltd. They sold a whole range of pork products, pies, sausages, black pudding, saveloy, polony and faggots. Their speciality was a thing called a 'Bath chap' which was the cheek, or jowl, of a pig. It was boiled or baked and covered in breadcrumbs. Their products were always of the top quality and the business was well respected. They had shops in Bath and Chippenham but most of their trade was supplying other businesses throughout the South West. Deliveries were made in a fleet of distinctive green vans bearing the company logo. Founder, George, died in 1914 and was succeeded by his brother Fred. When he died in 1935, Edward took over. In the early 1900s they had premises in Victoria Street, Temple Street, Broad Plain and Old Bread Street. The Broad Plain building received some damage during the Blitz of 3 January 1941 but was not destroyed. By 1972 the Old Bread Street buildings were empty and by 1975 the office premises were demolished to make way for the offices now fronting Temple Way. The business was sold in 1973 when all their shops were closed.

four

The Batch

All: The Primitive Methodist
Chapel at Nos 28–30 Midland
Road. The first Primitive
Methodist Chapel to be built
in Bristol, around 1850, it
is situated between Horton
Street and Midland Street in
Midland Road. Its name was
changed to Ebenezer Primitive
Methodist Chapel in the 1930s
and in the '40s it became the
Christadelphian Hall. The west
front is neo-Norman. It has a
zigzag-style door with three
unusual windows above it with
circular metal glazing bars.
There are no side windows. The
interior has very heavy wooden
galleries and an arched, flattened
barrel-vault ceiling. After it
closed in the 1950s it had several
owners, but since 1986 has been
an architectural salvage business.

Christopher Thomas & Son. The first soap works at Broad Plain were erected in 1784 and owned by the Fripp family who had been in business since 1745. The Thomas family joined the company in 1841, when the Fripp family retired. In 1856 the company became Christopher Thomas & Bros. From then on many changes and alterations were made to the buildings. In 1882 the towers of the Palazzo Vecchio in Florence became the inspiration for the towers that disguise the chimneys.

The golden years of the company were 1856-89. The crisis years were from 1889-1914. It was at this time that W.H. Lever took over and the factory was entirely reconstructed. During the war, components for the Beaufighter Plane and parts for the Lee Enfield rifle were produced here, along with potato powder.

Competition and politics resulted in its closure in 1953. Three-hundred and fifty-five employees lost their jobs; a far cry from the days when you could see the company doctor, take holidays, outings and a pension, when you were called by your surname and long service was the norm. The factory was sold to three buyers, Gardiner, Son & Co. Ltd, Rediffusion and Hardware (Bristol) Ltd.

Above and below: One of Bristol's oldest industries, Christopher Thomas & Bros Ltd, soap and candle works at Broad Plain. Established in 1745.

Above, left: Puritan Soap was launched in 1898. Thomas's spent £175 per month on advertising. The gift scheme started in 1904 and continued until 1939. The company had a gift shop at the Bristol Tramways Centre.

Above, right: The inscription on this bust reads: Christopher James Thomas, representative for St Philip and St Jacob Without on the town council for thirty-eight years from 1845-78. Mayor 1871. Born 1807. Died 1894. This bust was presented to St Philips Library on 6 February 1897, where it is kept to this day.

Hardware Ltd, Old Bread Street. Once part of Thomas's soap factory, it is built from pennant stone with red-brick bands and has five arched bays on the ground floor crowned with friezes. The first floor has ten arched windows. Empty for over thirty years, the façade has now been incorporated into a new development.

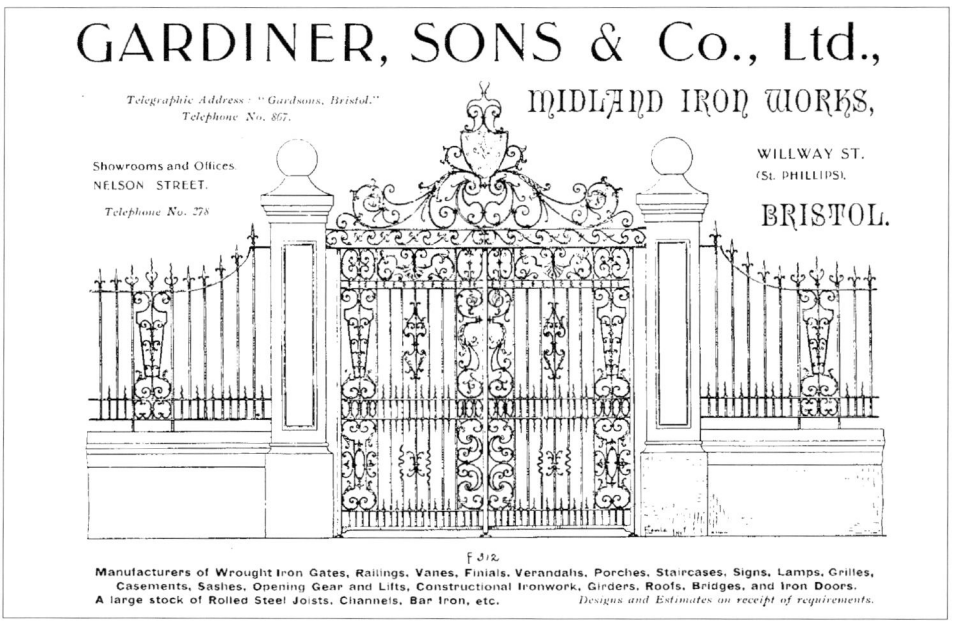

Advertisement for Gardiner, Sons & Co. Ltd, *c.* 1908.

Gardiner's was started by Zacharias Cartwright in 1825. They were blacksmiths, engineers, ironmongers and cabinet makers. The great engineer Isambard Kingdom Brunel bought his drawing instruments from them. These are now held at Bristol University library. After Zacharias's death his nephew, Emmanuel Chillcott, acquired the firm. In 1860 he was joined as a partner by Alfred Gardiner who, a few years later, brought in his two sons John and Thomas. During those years they moved from John Street and Tower Lane into an old boot factory in Nelson Street, and had another premises in All Saints Street. In 1897 they opened The Midland Iron Works in Willway Street, just off Midland Road, supplying shop signs, shop fronts and steel work for buildings. They were busy during the Second World War producing important parts for the war effort. These works stood where Gardiner's car park stands today. They took over part of the old soap factory in 1953 where they still trade today.

NELSON STREET

BUILDERS & FURNISHING IRONMONGERY
HEATING, COOKING & LIGHTING
APPLIANCES
BATH ROOM & SANITARY FITTINGS

One of the Largest Stocks & Showrooms in the Kingdom

MIDLAND IRONWORKS
WILLWAY STREET, ST. PHILIPS

CONSTRUCTIONAL STEEL WORK
ORNAMENTAL IRONWORK
GATES, RAILINGS, PORTICOS
HANDPOWER LIFTS
STEEL SASHES & CASEMENTS
OPENING GEAR & LEADED GLAZING
FIREPROOF DOORS & STAIRCASES
STRONG ROOM SHELVES & FITTINGS

Advertisement for Gardiner, Sons & Co. Ltd, Nelson Street, *c.* 1925.

The complete & varied equipment of the works gives unusual facilities for executing special made metal work of all descriptions

Above: Harold P. Williams, groceries, dairy products and provisions, stood at No. 17 New Thomas Street. On the wall to the left of the door is a mosaic tiled design featuring two cows and the words Axe Vale Dairy. The building was demolished in the 1950s and replaced by a garage. The Pride of the Forest public house (below) stood on the opposite corner.

Left: The Pride of the Forest, No. 18 Unity Street at its junction with New Thomas Street. Only the outer shell remains today, with the wording removed. It is now part of the outer wall of Gardiner's garden centre.

Unity Chapel, Midland Road. A young Cornishman and local evangelist named John Victor commenced open-air preaching in this city slum area in a small house in Goat Alley in 1850. Within five years the congregation had outgrown the building and a small chapel was built in Unity Street seating 200 people. Soon they needed a bigger church and in 1862 Unity Chapel was erected in Midland Road with seating for 800 people. A large schoolroom was added in 1865 and, later, galleries capable of seating an extra 400 people were added. George Muller who founded Muller's Orphanage was one of the preachers who visited this chapel. By 1943, due to industrialisation and people moving away, membership declined. The chapel was sold in 1946, although the schoolroom continued to be used for a short while. The money from the sale was used to fund a chapel at Lockleaze. The building had several owners in the following years, the last being Sampson's Cycles. It was demolished in January 2002.

The chapel as owned by Sampson's Cycles. The Midland Inn stands almost next door.

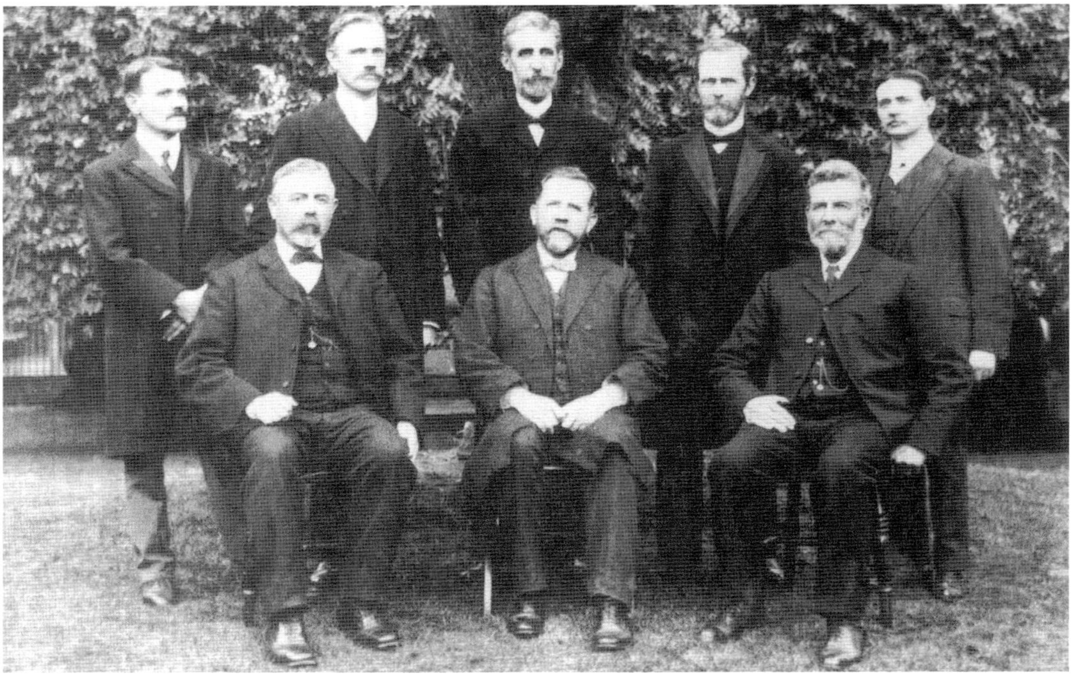

Above: Members of the chapel deaconate. From left to right, standing: Thomas Hancock, J. Henry Payne, W.A. Coxall, Alf D.H. Fox, William A. Iles. Seated: Henry A. Burnell (treasurer), Alf Dennes (secretary), Reuben Martin. Absent from this picture were Albert Dainton and William Oatway.

Below, left: Pastor W.J. Morgan, the first pastor of the chapel.
Below, right: Unity Chapel gave this splendid certificate to John Henry Payne when he emigrated to Australia in 1912.

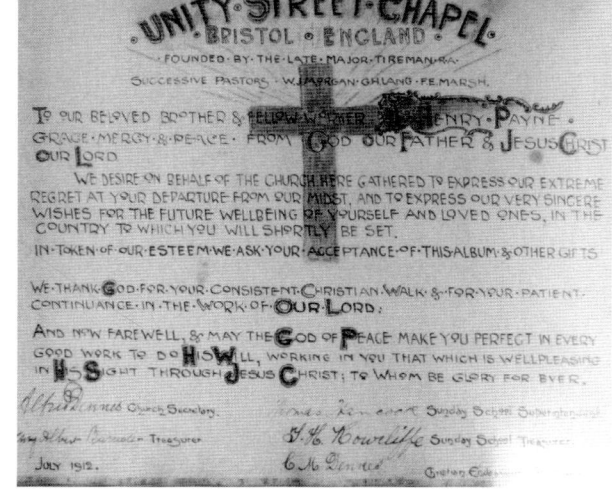

St Philips station opened on 2 May 1870. It was a small building quite cheaply constructed from wood with a glass canopy. Owned and built by the Midland Railway Co., later known as the London, Midland and Scottish Railway Co., in its heyday it carried passengers between Bath, Gloucester, Yate, Fishponds and Mangotsfield, which helped to relieve congestion at Temple Meads. Its thirteen trains a day brought many workers into the city. It was very busy in the morning and evening rush. This would only decrease after the blitz of 1941 when Castle Street was destroyed and Old Market started its decline.

It had just one platform with a locomotive run-round loop. In later years the waiting room was often used by staff for the storage of documents. On 21 September 1953 the station closed. Until that time the whole of the area between Waterloo Road and Kingsland Road consisted of the station, including the goods station, the railways athletic and social club, William Burgess freight carriers, and the upper railway wharf. Ten years later only the goods station along with Thomas Silvey and A.S. Hill coal merchants remained. Some evidence of the railway could still be seen until 1975, but by this time the site was a car and lorry park. It then became a car auction business and was eventually completely redeveloped as an industrial unit.

A Simple Poem Remembering My Dad

Privileged was I, some seventy-five years back,
My hand clasped my Dad's, as we walked the tracks,
Metal gleaming, whistles screaming,
Unofficial trips of school child's dreaming.
Through great black hole of Bath Road sheds,
Dim with smoke, dust, dirt, oiled heads,
Repair, repair, unhinged fire door,
Shuddering engine and warped plate floor.
Mops a swishing, buckets clanging,
Carriage cleaners, tongues a wagging,
Permanent smell of oily rags,
Whizzing wheels shriek as I cling to my Dad.
Hiss of steam, wheeltappers tapping,
Trucks, tarpaulin, nervously flapping,
Bristol engine sheds, my Dad's a fitter,
Works hard to accommodate daytime tripper.
Handle the jack boys, tow the line,
She's due at Kings Cross at quarter to nine,
Brunel smiles down, his stations no dream,
Neither was mine, in that old age of steam.

(W.H. Lucas, 1930)

St Philips goods shed. The station occupied only a small part of this extensive site, which was dominated by a large shed which boasted elaborate facilities for the handling of goods. It was badly damaged by the Bristol Blitz in 1941, when its distinctive multi-span roof was completely destroyed. This was never replaced, leaving the yards exposed. The goods yard finally closed on 1 April 1963 as part of British Rail cutbacks.

Jacob Street, Midland Railway Co. stables. The yard had stables to the right and to the left a wooden gangway, known as creeps, which took the horses to stables on an upper level. There were entrances in both Unity Street and Jacob Street.

Right: An engine waits at Day's Road as a double-decker bus crosses the bridge, 1964.

Below: Advertisements for E. Sohier, *c.* 1879, and Samuel Wallis, *c.* 1915.

Left: W.J. Rogers' Ltd, delivery vehicles.

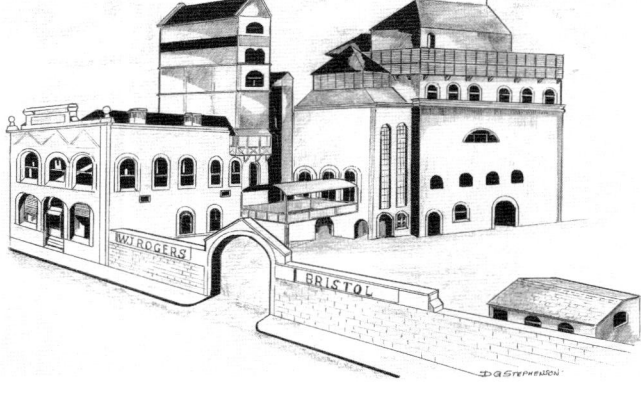

W.J. Rogers' brewery, from a drawing by Dennis Stephenson.

Rogers' brewery. There had been a brewery in Jacob Street from at least 1845. John Rogers was the first member of the family to operate there. He had another building at No. 90 Old Market Street which he used as offices. His son, William John Rogers, would take over and make many alterations over the years to the brewery, which was designed by William Bruce Gingell in the well known Bristol Byzantine style of architecture.

The brewery used the Burton system of brewing. The tower, constructed at great expense, was 100ft high, 40ft in length and 20ft wide. The water used came from a well thought to be 300ft in depth, containing water of fine quality. As a rule, hard water was used for ales and soft water for porter. The brewery had its own works department in the large courtyard, coopers' shops, cask repairers and cask stores. There were also buildings of three or four storeys containing twelve malting floors and six kilns. Cheese Lane was where they stored the casks of ale and beer. While building the brewery, part of an old Benedictine priory was discovered containing many stone coffins.

Many of the houses in Jacob Street were owned by the brewery and used by the workers. In the 1920s they took over the Anglo Brewing Co., J. & T. Usher and W.G. Reynolds, Bath. They employed around 230 people at this time.
In 1935 H. & G. Simmonds gained control of Rogers' brewery. Brewing continued until the early 1950s, and bottling until the late 1950s. At the same time, houses in Jacob Street were being demolished.

In 1960 Courage's took over the brewery. The Co-operative Society built a new grocery distribution depot (1962-73) on part of the site, but because of problems with lorries damaging the walls of St Philip and St Jacob church they moved to Whitby Road.

Temple way was built in 1968 cutting right through Jacob Street. The *Evening Post* building is on part of the old site. The only building left standing is now called Company House. It was at one time owned by Casey's Camping.

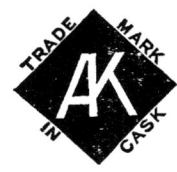

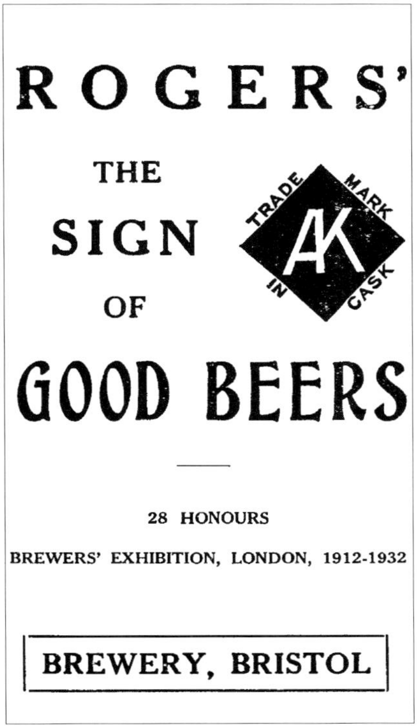
ROGERS'
THE
SIGN
OF
TRADE MARK
AK
IN CASK
GOOD BEERS
28 HONOURS
BREWERS' EXHIBITION, LONDON, 1912-1932
BREWERY, BRISTOL

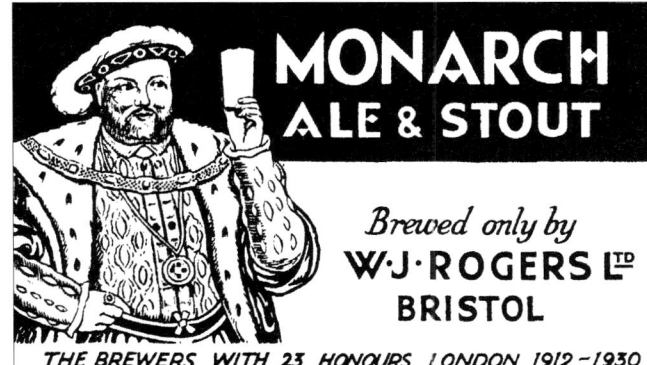

MONARCH
ALE & STOUT
Brewed only by
W·J·ROGERS LTD
BRISTOL
THE BREWERS WITH 23 HONOURS LONDON 1912-1930

Left and above: Rogers' pubs were distinguished by a large barrel-shaped lamp of coloured glass which stood over the door. They used the symbol of a red diamond for their famous AK Bitter Ale.

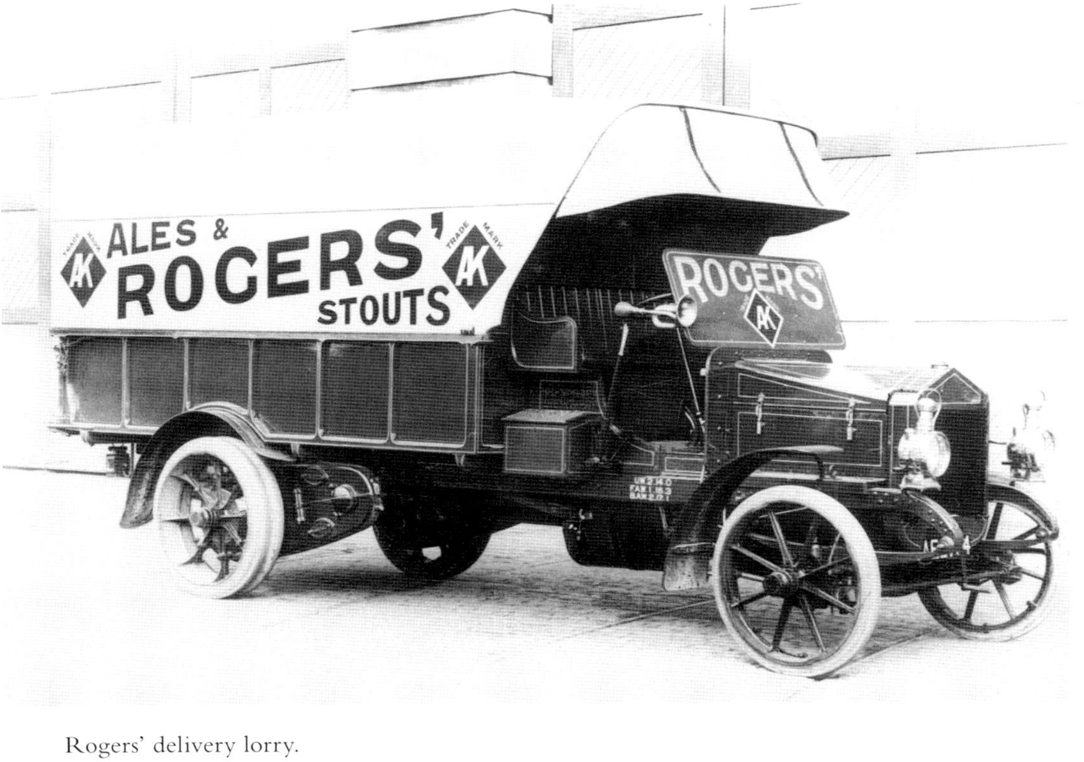
ALES &
ROGERS'
STOUTS
AK
ROGERS'

Rogers' delivery lorry.

The Francis burial ground, in between West Street and Waterloo Road. These bones were unearthed when the building, now known as the hide market, in West Street was being constructed. They belong to the Francis burial ground which opened in the early 1800s and was privately owned. It measured 62.5m long and 12.5m wide. The entrance was in Waterloo Road. A high wall surrounded it, some of which remains today. You can clearly see where doorways and windows once were. It closed around 1854.

It would seem that no record exists of who is buried there, except for a letter from a solicitor to the family of Mr Daniel Bowry, which states that he was present at a burial in June 1833. In 1853 the *Bristol Times* wrote that between two- and three-dozen burials took place there every Sunday.

A brass works was eventually constructed on the site. It then became part of the hide market and later a wastepaper yard. Local businesses alerted police in the 1980s when bones were discovered close to the surface by workmen. Pieces of burial cloth were also visible. The intended building on this area of land was cancelled and it was turned into a car park

If you look closely at the boundary wall you can see the outline of an arched doorway to the Francis burial ground.

Above and below: British Paper (Waste) Ltd, West Street, Old Market, in the 1980s, with an entrance for its vehicles in Waterloo Road. The business was owned by the Edwards brothers who later moved to Netham Road. Their vehicles were very familiar around the streets of Bristol.

Left: A.E. Phipps, No. 29 Midland Road, sometime in the 1920s. The advertisements for Spratt's pet foods were painted by hand. This building still stands today.

Below: The Midland Inn, first mentioned in 1869 but later changing its name to the Midland Railway Inn. The landlord for many years was Thomas Foxwell. The building, which probably should have been listed, was demolished in October 1998.

Right and below: Two advertisements taken from local church magazines of the 1930s.

KINGSLAND ROAD

Midland Road to Silverthorne Lane

19. Fowler, Mrs Caroline
23. Fred England Ltd. Potato importers
Barton Road and Windsor Place intersect
London Midland & Scottish Railway Bridge
55. Humphries, Mrs Harriet
57. Ackerman, Alfred
59. Tarring, Thomas Hy
61. Coles, Mrs Alice
63. Jarrett Hy Charles. Cycle dealer
65. Chiddy, Mrs Florence Ada. Butcher
67. Jones, George Daniel
69. Lancaster, Alfred Hardiman. Shopkeeper
71. Cox, Miss Kathleen
73. Davies, Cornelius Jason
75. Wolfe, Frederick Charles
77. Nethercott, Thomas
Shaftesbury Hall & Congreational Mission Room –
    Hy M. Harris sec. Shaftesbury Crusade (incorporated)
    Reading & Recreation Rooms – Hy M. Harris sec.
Oxford Street intersects
149. Berkeley Castle (William T. Rowland)
Dibbles Court intersects
Gas Lane intersects
Here cross over Kingsland Road Siding
Burnett, Thomas. Wagon repairer
Cambrian Wagon Co. Wagon repairers
Marcroft Wagon Ltd. Wagon repairers
Hunter Thomas Ltd. Wagon repairers
Renwick, Wilson & Dobson. Coal merchants (depot)
Wagon Repairs Ltd. Wagon repairers
130. Victoria Tavern (Albert Fifoot)
Queen Victoria Street intersects
128. Tomlin, William. Shopkeeper
116. Parsons, Ernest. Junior shopkeeper

Days Road intersects
104. The George (Robert Alden)
102. Spickett, Mrs Florence Elizabeth. Hardware dealer
100. Hadden, Alfred. Hairdresser
98. Box, Fred. Baker
96. Moore, Frederick. Greengrocer
94. Town Sub-post office and M.O. office. Miss Ivy Doris
    Taylor, sub-postmistress
94. Taylor, Miss Ivy Doris. Laundry agent
88. Hunt, Jason Alfred. Butcher
80 & 78. Parker, William. Potato fryer
Sussex Street intersects
74. Batt, Hy Thomas. Charles who. Tobacconist
68. Edwards, Robert. Junior butcher
66. White, Mrs Kate. Beer retailer
64. Pullin, Joseph J. Wireless supplies dealer
60. O'Dowd, Edward Paul M.B.Ch.B.Edin. Physician
    & surgeon (surgery)
54 & 56. Bristol Co-operative Society Ltd (Branch no. 9)
    (grocery dept.)
52. Cartwright, Mrs Mary Jane
50. Endicott, Mrs Eugene
48. Burgess, Jason
46. Cox, Hy George
44. Youens, Mrs
42. Board, Miss Joyce
40. Hooper, William Charles
Princess Street intersects
LMS Railway Bridge
Railway Terrace intersects
Kingsland Congregational Church
30. Smith, Edward Thomas. Boot repairer
York Street intersects
22. Taylor, Mrs P.
20. Johns, Thomas. Decorator
GWR Good Depot

MIDLAND ROAD

Top of Old Market Street to Kingsland Road

7. Taylor, Jason Thomas. Fishmonger
9 & 11. Palmer & Verren. Wholesale confectioners
13. Gladstone, Mrs E.L. Tobacconist
15. Parlour, Ernest Hewer. Butcher
17. Greyhound Inn (Mrs Florence. M. Francis)
19. Shipway, William George. Confectioner
21. Lewis, Bertie. Fried fish dealer
23 & 25. Staddon, Mrs Beatrce. Refreshment rooms
27. Nicholls, Arthur Claude. Refreshment rooms
29. Hallett, Bob. Corn dealer
31. Holmes, Walter. Greengrocer
33. Newbury, Alfred. Refreshment rooms
35. Arnold, Miss Lily. Draper
37. Rennolds, Mrs Mabel. Tobacconist
39. Swan Inn (Jason Frederick Jnr. Feltham)
Waterloo Road intersects
St Philips LM & S Railway Station
LM&S Railway Goods Station
LM&S (Bristol) Athletic & Social Club (St Philips
    Goods Station) J.W. Archibald hon. sec.)
LM&S Railway. St Philips Goods Station Rifle Club.
    J.W. Wildgoose hon. sec.
Burgess, William (Bristol Ltd). Carriers
Upper Railway Wharf
Kingsland Road intersects
Here cross over

56. Page, Mrs Helena Caroline. Shopkeeper
54. Boniface, William
Louisa Street intersects
48. Bland, Mrs Annie. China dealer
46. Hughes, Frank Sidney. Hairdresser
44. Exon, William Parker
40. The Apple Tree (Mrs Violet May Sherman)
Midland Street intersects
34. Daniels, Charles. Greengrocer
32. Silvey, Thomas Ltd. Coal merchants (wholesale office)
Christadelphian Hall
26. Sutton, Charles. Greengrocer
Horton Street intersects
22. Moger. Frederick. Rd. Fried fish dealer
20. Wyatt, Mrs Agnes S. Coffee tavern
Humphrys & Oakes. Brass founders
Willway Street intersects
14. Midland Inn (Mrs G. Lilian May Stenner)
Unity Chapel
Unity Street intersects

Above: Arthur Thomas Poeton, electro plater, had premises at Tower Hill at its junction with Marybush Lane from 1905-63. It was also known as the Tower Plating Works. They moved to Whitehouse Street, Bedminster, and then to Gloucester, where they still trade.

Opposite: Kingsland Road and Midland Road listings, adapted from *Kelly's Directory*, 1944.

CART, VAN, GIG, SHOW HARNESS.

HOME-MADE BOOTS. ARMY BOOTS. LEGGINGS.

J. J. JACOBS, Harness, Saddlery, Boot & Leather Merchant,
3 & 4 PASSAGE STREET, BRISTOL.

Above: J.J. Jacobs, Nos 3 and 4 Passage Street, were saddlers, boot and shoe manufacturers from the late 1890s to the 1960s. John Jacobs ran the business, then his wife Ellen, followed by their daughter Miss Dora Jacobs. The shop was opposite the Central Health Clinic, a few doors away from the King's Head public house.

Left: The Prince of Wales, No. 8 Tower Hill. In 1978 this public house, Veale's fishing tackle shop and the Spring Chicken café were purchased for demolition. The site now forms part of the Castlegate office complex.

The district of St Philip and St Jacob. St Philip and St Jacob was originally a religious house or priory of the order of St Benedict which was founded before 1200. Initially outside the city walls, it was within the county of Gloucestershire. However, the city administration was determined that they should be in control of an area so close to their boundary. Thus in 1373 a city charter was granted as part of the extension of the city to the east, thus Old Market and the area around St Philip and St Jacob would now be part of Bristol, but still mainly owned by the church. This only changed when Henry VIII made himself head of the church in 1535 and sold off those lands.

In subsequent years the ancient parish of St Philip and St Jacob was to be divided and subdivided. The first division was in 1720 when the parish of St Philip and St Jacob Outer was created to the east of the church itself, from West Street to the Bitton parish boundary. Part of this outer was renamed Bristol St George in 1756, the remaining part being renamed St Philip and St Jacob Inner. From then on new parishes were created as the population grew and new churches were built.

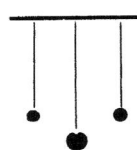

Above and below: Raselle's, No. 46 Old Market Street. In 1894 Amos Raselle took over this pawnbroker's shop from the Lyddon family. He ran it until the 1950s when the Fowler family took over. Benjamin Price recalled Amos Raselle as being about 5ft tall with a little goatee beard, who looked like King Edward VII. He always wore an Astrakhan coat and hat and was known as a friend of the poor. Every year he gave a considerable amount of prizes to Emmanuel School, usually books for the annual prize giving. In 1938 Moseley's black shirts rented a shop in West Street. Although Amos Raselle was Jewish and a soft target, he was respected by the local community and no one would harm him.

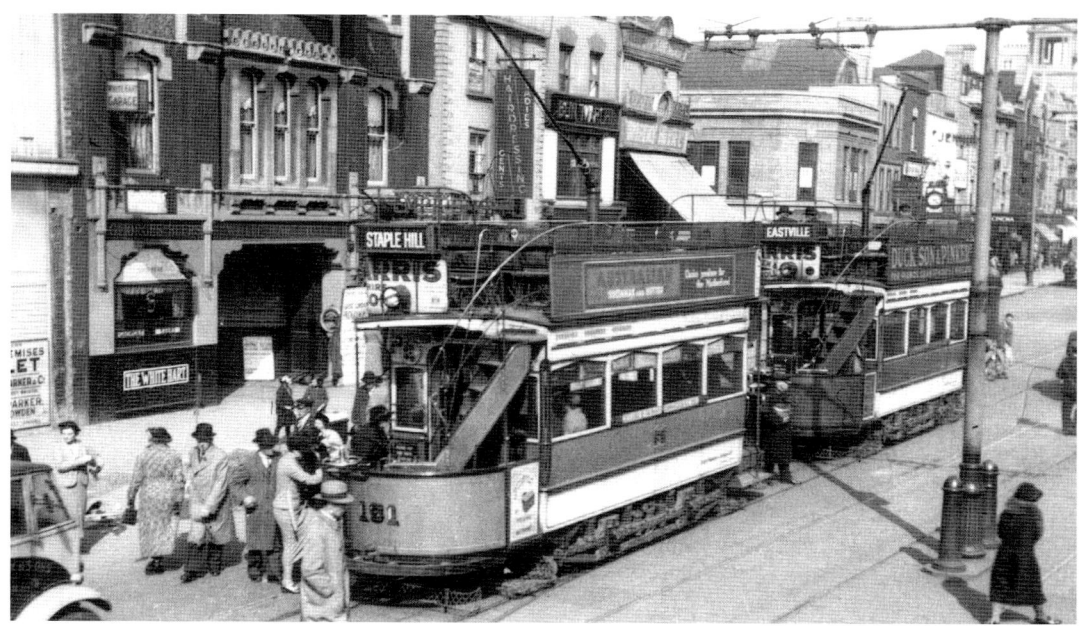

Old Market, April 1935. Trams are going to Eastville and Staple Hill. The White Hart pub is to the left and the Central Hall is in the distance.

Old Market Street. The people of The Dings would have known this street very well as it was once a bustling, busy street leading to Castle Street, the heart of Bristol. This part of Old Market has now been replaced by the Temple Way roundabout and subway.

Other local titles published by Tempus

Kingswood and Two Mile Hill

Jill Willmott

Kingswood and Two Mile Hill was formerly an important coal-mining and shoe-manufacturing district and this book highlights the changes and developments to local schools, shops, churches, hospitals, pubs and cinemas (including the Regent Cinema, which opened in 1912), and to the area's industrial scene, including ironmongers, blacksmiths and forges, as well as the larger factories of Douglas Engineering and Langridges Corset Factory.

0 7524 3311 3

Crews Hole, St George and Speedwell

Dave Stephenson, Dave Cheesley, Jill Willmott and Andy Jones

Illustrated with over 200 archive pictures, this collection evocatively captures the histories of Netham, Crews Hole, St George and Speedwell in east Bristol. Snapshots of everyday life combine with vistas of the industries upon which these communities relied, particularly the collieries and chemical works whose chimneys towered over this area of the city. This fascinating volume shows the great changes which have taken place in commerce, heavy industry, transport and residential areas.

0 7524 2948 5

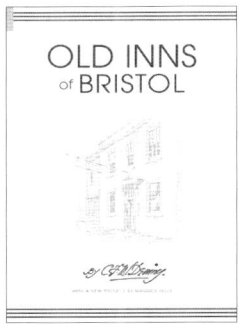

Old Inns of Bristol

CFW Dening, with a new preface by Maurice Fells

Old Inns of Bristol is a fascinating guide to the historic pubs in the city. First published in 1943, the original book is reproduced here, along with an updated preface by local writer and broadcaster Maurice Fells. This book offers the reader an insight into the life of pubs past and present, from the oddly named Rhubarb Tavern to the dockside pubs with their stories of pirates and smugglers.

0 7524 3475 6

Old Market, Newtown, Lawrence Hill and Moorfields

David Stephenson, Andy Jones, David Cheesley and Ernie Haste

This selection of over 200 old photographs recalls life in Bristol before the huge development projects saw streets and communities vanish to make way for ring roads, underpasses and roundabouts. Visit Angel's Café in Old Market, the Empire Palace of Varieties where many stars from Gracie Fields to Harry Houdini walked the boards, and remember the trams moving up and down in rush-hour.

0 7524 2618 4

If you are interested in purchasing other books published by Tempus, or in case you have difficulty finding any Tempus books in your local bookshop, you can also place orders directly through our website

www.tempus-publishing.com